HOLT Elements of Language

FOURTH COURSE

Chapter Tests in Standardized Test Formats

- Reading
- Writing
- Sentences and Paragraphs
- Grammar, Usage, Mechanics

HOLT, RINEHART AND WINSTON

A Harcourt Education Company

Orlando • Austin • New York • San Diego • London

Copyright © by Holt, Rinehart and Winston

All rights reserved. No part of this publication may be reproduced or transmitted in any form or by any means, electronic or mechanical, including photocopy, recording, or any information storage and retrieval system, without permission in writing from the publisher.

Teachers using ELEMENTS OF LANGUAGE may photocopy blackline masters in complete pages in sufficient quantities for classroom use only and not for resale.

ELEMENTS OF LANGUAGE, HOLT, HRW, and the **"Owl Design"** are trademarks licensed to Holt, Rinehart and Winston, registered in the United States of America and/or other jurisdictions.

Printed in the United States of America

If you have received these materials as examination copies free of charge, Holt, Rinehart and Winston retains title to the materials and they may not be resold. Resale of examination copies is strictly prohibited.

Possession of this publication in print format does not entitle users to convert this publication, or any portion of it, into electronic format.

ISBN 978-0-03-099315-2
ISBN 0-03-099315-6

1 2 3 4 5 6 018 13 12 11 10 09 08 07

Table of Contents

About These Tests vi

Grammar, Usage, and Mechanics

for Part 1
(Student Edition pp. 46–487)

for **Chapter 1: Parts of Speech Overview** 1

for **Chapter 2: The Parts of a Sentence** 3

for **Chapter 3: The Phrase** 5

for **Chapter 4: The Clause** 7

for **Chapter 5: Agreement** 9

for **Chapter 6: Using Pronouns Correctly** 11

for **Chapter 7: Using Verbs Correctly** 13

for **Chapter 8: Using Modifiers Correctly** 15

for **Chapter 9: A Glossary of Usage** 17

for **Chapter 10: Capitalization** 19

for **Chapter 11: Punctuation**
End Marks and Commas 21

for **Chapter 12: Punctuation**
Semicolons and Colons 23

for **Chapter 13: Punctuation**
Italics, Quotation Marks, and Ellipsis Points 25

for **Chapter 14: Punctuation**
Apostrophes, Hyphens, Dashes, Parentheses, Brackets 27

for **Chapter 15: Spelling** 29

for **Chapter 16: Correcting Common Errors** 31

Table of Contents (continued)

Sentences and Paragraphs

for Part 2
(Student Edition
pp. 488–551)

for **Chapter 17: Writing Complete Sentences** **33**

for **Chapter 18: Writing Effective Sentences** **36**

for **Chapter 19: Understanding Paragraphs and Compositions** **41**

Communications

for Part 3
(Student Edition
pp. 552–877)

for **Chapter 20: Narration/Description**
Reflecting on Experiences
- Reading Workshop **45**
- Writing Workshop **47**

for **Chapter 21: Exposition**
Exploring Comparisons and Contrasts
- Reading Workshop **50**
- Writing Workshop **52**

for **Chapter 22: Exposition**
Examining Causes and Effects
- Reading Workshop **54**
- Writing Workshop **56**

for **Chapter 23: Exposition**
Analyzing Problems
- Reading Workshop **59**
- Writing Workshop **61**

for **Chapter 24: Exposition**
Analyzing a Short Story
- Reading Workshop **64**
- Writing Workshop **66**

for **Chapter 25: Exposition**
Sharing Research Results
- Reading Workshop **69**
- Writing Workshop **72**

for **Chapter 26: Persuasion**
Persuading Others
- Reading Workshop **75**
- Writing Workshop **77**

for **Chapter 27: Persuasion**
Using Persuasion in Advertising
- Reading Workshop **80**
- Writing Workshop **82**

Table of Contents *(continued)*

Answer Sheets

Correcting Common Errors Standardized Test Answer Sheet 85
Answer Sheet 1: Grammar, Usage, and Mechanics 86
Answer Sheet 2: Sentences and Paragraphs 87
Answer Sheet 3: Sentences and Paragraphs 88
Answer Sheet 4: Reading and Writing Workshops 89
Answer Sheet 5: Reading and Writing Workshops 90
Answer Sheet 6: Reading and Writing Workshops 91

FOR THE TEACHER

About These Tests

Every chapter in your *Elements of Language* Student Edition has an accompanying Chapter Test in a standardized test format. You will recognize the formats of a wide variety of standardized tests. The *Chapter Tests in Standardized Test Formats* will not only allow you to assess student performance, they will familiarize students with a range of standardized tests and give them practice in test taking.

The Answer Keys for these tests are located on the *Teacher One Stop*™ **DVD-ROM with ExamView® Test Generator**.

**Part 1
Grammar, Usage, and Mechanics**

The Part 1 tests provide assessment for the rules and all key concepts taught in the grammar, usage, and mechanics chapters in the Student Edition. Students demonstrate their mastery of the instruction by answering multiple-choice items that test their knowledge of the content covered in the Student Edition.

**Part 2
Sentences and Paragraphs**

The Part 2 tests provide assessment for each major section within the Sentences and Paragraphs chapters. Students answer multiple-choice items about the content covered in the Student Edition. These items test students' mastery of the key concepts taught in the chapters.

**Part 3
Communications**

The Part 3 tests include assessment for both the Reading and the Writing Workshops. You may choose to administer the Reading and Writing Workshop tests separately or as one test after students have completed the chapter.

In the **Reading Workshop** test, students read a passage and respond to multiple-choice items. The passage is in the mode that students have just studied, and the multiple-choice items assess students' proficiency in the chapter's Reading Skill and Reading Focus.

The **Writing Workshop** test provides a passage containing problems or errors in several or all of the following areas: content, organization, style, grammar and usage, and mechanics. Students demonstrate their understanding of the mode of writing and their revising and proofreading skills by responding to multiple-choice items. Students identify elements of the mode of writing, restructure segments of the passage, add clarifying statements, refine language, and correct errors in the passage.

Answer Sheets

Answer sheets are provided in the back of the booklet. The answer sheets correspond to the letter answer options designated by a particular standardized test. Use the following chart to help you determine which answer sheet to use for each test. Students may use the **Correcting Common Errors Standardized Test Answer Sheet** for the **Grammar and Usage Test** and **Mechanics Test** in the Student Edition.

FOR THE TEACHER

About These Tests *(continued)*

Chapter	Answer Sheet
Chapters 1–16	Answer Sheet 1
Student Edition Chapter 16	Common Errors Standardized Test Answer Sheet
Chapter 17	Answer Sheet 3
Chapter 18	Answer Sheet 2
Chapter 19	Answer Sheet 2
Chapter 20: Reading Workshop	Answer Sheet 4
Writing Workshop	Answer Sheet 5
Chapter 21: Reading Workshop	Answer Sheet 5
Writing Workshop	Answer Sheet 4
Chapter 22: Reading Workshop	Answer Sheet 4
Writing Workshop	Students answer on test.
Chapter 23: Reading Workshop	Students answer on test.
Writing Workshop	Answer Sheet 4
Chapter 24: Reading Workshop	Answer Sheet 4
Writing Workshop	Answer Sheet 5
Chapter 25: Reading Workshop	Answer Sheet 5
Writing Workshop	Answer Sheet 4
Chapter 26: Reading Workshop	Answer Sheet 6
Writing Workshop	Students answer on test.
Chapter 27: Reading Workshop	Answer Sheet 5
Writing Workshop	Answer Sheet 5

Teacher One Stop™ DVD-ROM with ExamView® Test Generator

All of the questions in this booklet are available on the *Teacher One Stop™* DVD-ROM with ExamView® Test Generator. Use the ExamView Test Generator to customize any of the tests in this booklet and create a test unique to your classroom situation. You can then print a test or post it to the *Holt Online Assessment* area at **my.hrw.com**.

Holt Online Assessment

Holt Online Assessment provides an easy way to administer tests to your students online. Students can log on to **my.hrw.com** to take a test that you have created using the ExamView Test Generator, or you can assign one of the tests already available on the site.

for **CHAPTER 1** pages 48–79

CHAPTER TEST

Parts of Speech Overview: Identification and Function

DIRECTIONS Read each sentence below, and look at the underlined word or words. Then, choose the part of speech of the underlined word or words.

EXAMPLE

1. The <u>gong</u> is an important part of an orchestra's percussion section.
   A noun
   B pronoun
   C verb
   D adjective

   Answer (A) (B) (C) (D)

---

1. Zippers, which most people use <u>several</u> times each week, were not invented until 1893.
   A adverb
   B preposition
   C adjective
   D conjunction

2. Known for his inspiring paintings of laborers, Diego Rivera painted murals on buildings <u>in</u> several cities in Mexico and the United States.
   A interjection
   B adjective
   C preposition
   D pronoun

3. Machu Picchu <u>could have been discovered</u> centuries ago, but it was not found until 1911.
   A verb
   B pronoun
   C conjunction
   D adjective

4. <u>Wow!</u> That huge bullfrog just jumped two yards across the pond to another lily pad!
   A interjection
   B adverb
   C noun
   D preposition

5. <u>He</u> did research at the Hermitage Museum in St. Petersburg, Russia, for his art history book.
   A adjective
   B pronoun
   C conjunction
   D adverb

CHAPTER 1 | Parts of Speech Overview

1

for CHAPTER 1 pages 48–79 continued

CHAPTER TEST

6. To her disappointment, <u>neither</u> the daffodil <u>nor</u> the iris bulbs bloomed this spring.
   A   interjection
   B   conjunction
   C   adverb
   D   noun

7. For supper on Thursday, we <u>usually</u> have chicken and dumplings.
   A   adverb
   B   preposition
   C   interjection
   D   conjunction

8. <u>In addition to</u> acting, Sean also writes for the school newspaper, sings, and dances.
   A   pronoun
   B   adverb
   C   preposition
   D   verb

9. Blue, yellow, and red are considered primary colors, <u>because</u> every other color is derived from them.
   A   conjunction
   B   noun
   C   interjection
   D   adjective

10. Diwali, <u>which</u> is the Hindu festival of lights, occurs in late autumn.
    A   preposition
    B   pronoun
    C   adverb
    D   adjective

| NAME | CLASS | DATE | SCORE |

for CHAPTER 2 pages 80–109   **CHAPTER TEST**

The Parts of a Sentence: Subjects, Predicates, Complements

DIRECTIONS Read each sentence below. For items 1–6, choose the answer that tells in what way the underlined word or words are used in the sentence. For items 7–10, choose the answer that identifies the kind of sentence.

EXAMPLES

1. Did <u>you</u> know that a baptistery is part of a church?
   A verb
   B subject
   C direct object
   D predicate nominative

   Answer Ⓐ ●B Ⓒ Ⓓ

2. Lucinda, please hand me the TV remote control.
   A declarative
   B interrogative
   C imperative
   D exclamatory

   Answer Ⓐ Ⓑ ●C Ⓓ

---

1. During our trip to South America, my mother showed Hector and <u>me</u> the places where she lived in Venezuela and Ecuador.
   A direct object
   B predicate nominative
   C predicate adjective
   D indirect object

2. <u>The blue jay and its mate</u> are diving at my head because they are protecting a nest full of eggs.
   A indirect object
   B direct object
   C predicate nominative
   D subject

3. Were both of these songs <u>hits</u> last year?
   A subject
   B predicate adjective
   C direct object
   D predicate nominative

4. By using the omniscient point of view, an author <u>can reveal</u> and even comment on the private thoughts and emotions of characters.
   A predicate nominative
   B direct object
   C verb
   D indirect object

CHAPTER 2 | The Parts of a Sentence   3

for **CHAPTER 2** pages 80–109 continued   **CHAPTER TEST**

5. That volcano is no longer <u>active</u>.
   A verb
   B predicate adjective
   C subject
   D predicate nominative

6. Archaeologists and anthropologists still cannot answer this <u>question</u> precisely: When did people from Asia arrive on the North American continent?
   A predicate nominative
   B indirect object
   C direct object
   D predicate adjective

7. Did you know that Helena found several studies on butterflies' important role in pollination while she was searching the Internet?
   A declarative
   B interrogative
   C imperative
   D exclamatory

8. How naive Joe is to think he's an expert on subatomic particles after only one physics course!
   A declarative
   B interrogative
   C imperative
   D exclamatory

9. The space station *Mir*, which was built by the Russians, was in service until 2001.
   A declarative
   B interrogative
   C imperative
   D exclamatory

10. Explain what *sensibility* meant during the eighteenth century.
    A declarative
    B interrogative
    C imperative
    D exclamatory

| NAME | CLASS | DATE | SCORE |

for CHAPTER 3 pages 110–133

CHAPTER TEST

The Phrase: Prepositional, Verbal, and Appositive Phrases

DIRECTIONS Read each sentence below, and look at the underlined phrase. Then, choose the answer that identifies the type of phrase. Do not separately identify a prepositional phrase that is part of a larger phrase.

EXAMPLE

1. <u>During photosynthesis</u>, plants use carbon dioxide and give off oxygen.
   A prepositional phrase
   B participial phrase
   C gerund phrase
   D appositive phrase

   Answer

---

1. <u>To observe the fascinating world of creatures in a tide pool</u>, you must be quiet and still.
   A infinitive phrase
   B participial phrase
   C gerund phrase
   D prepositional phrase

2. <u>Roaming America's Southwest</u>, cowboys discovered ancient American Indian ruins.
   A gerund phrase
   B infinitive phrase
   C prepositional phrase
   D participial phrase

3. <u>Creating the movie *Citizen Kane*</u> was perhaps Orson Welles's greatest achievement.
   A participial phrase
   B gerund phrase
   C infinitive phrase
   D prepositional phrase

4. Ornate molding, <u>ornamental frames or strips</u>, decorates many buildings constructed during that era.
   A appositive phrase
   B gerund phrase
   C prepositional phrase
   D participial phrase

5. Some arias, or solos, <u>in Wolfgang Amadeus Mozart's opera *The Magic Flute*</u> feature extremely high notes.
   A gerund phrase
   B participial phrase
   C infinitive phrase
   D prepositional phrase

CHAPTER 3 | The Phrase

5

6. This summer we're traveling <u>by car</u> to visit Revolutionary War sites throughout the East Coast.
   A   prepositional phrase
   B   participial phrase
   C   gerund phrase
   D   appositive phrase

7. <u>To walk along Hadrian's Wall</u>, which the Romans built in England during the second century A.D., is a remarkable experience.
   A   participial phrase
   B   gerund phrase
   C   infinitive phrase
   D   prepositional phrase

8. <u>Exercising too much or in the wrong way</u> can cause muscle strain.
   A   gerund phrase
   B   appositive phrase
   C   prepositional phrase
   D   participial phrase

9. <u>Dressed in a white, sequined tutu</u>, the ballerina looked like a sparkling snowflake.
   A   participial phrase
   B   gerund phrase
   C   infinitive phrase
   D   prepositional phrase

10. "<u>Hearing Miles Davis play his trumpet</u> was the highlight of my teenage years," said my grandfather.
   A   appositive phrase
   B   gerund phrase
   C   prepositional phrase
   D   participial phrase

NAME _____ CLASS _____ DATE _____ SCORE _____

for **CHAPTER 4** pages 134–153

CHAPTER TEST

The Clause: Independent Clauses and Subordinate Clauses

DIRECTIONS Read each sentence below. For items 1–6, choose the answer that identifies the type of clause underlined in the sentence. For items 7–10, choose the answer that identifies the kind of sentence structure.

EXAMPLE

1. Chipping away rock, <u>the paleontologist discovered a dinosaur bone</u>.
   A independent clause
   B adverb clause
   C adjective clause
   D noun clause

   Answer

2. The piece of petrified wood on display in the natural history museum is beautiful.
   A compound sentence
   B simple sentence
   C complex sentence
   D compound-complex sentence

   Answer

---

1. El Greco was the artist <u>who painted the famous View of Toledo in the 1600s</u>.
   A independent clause
   B adverb clause
   C adjective clause
   D noun clause

2. Javier has written an essay about <u>how his family moved from Guatemala to the United States in 1997</u>.
   A independent clause
   B adverb clause
   C adjective clause
   D noun clause

3. <u>Before Catherine did research on the Internet</u>, she learned how to use different search engines.
   A independent clause
   B adverb clause
   C adjective clause
   D noun clause

4. While hiking in the Rocky Mountains, <u>Eric saw three black bears, an eagle, and one family of deer</u>.
   A independent clause
   B adverb clause
   C adjective clause
   D noun clause

5. The science teacher <u>who taught me about the electromagnetic spectrum</u> is Dr. Wong.
   A independent clause
   B adverb clause
   C adjective clause
   D noun clause

CHAPTER 4 | The Clause

CHAPTER TEST

for CHAPTER 4 pages 134–153 continued

6. So that the habits of wild bears could be tracked, the biologist attached tags to the cubs' ears.
   A   independent clause
   B   adverb clause
   C   adjective clause
   D   noun clause

7. After it emerged from its cocoon, the monarch butterfly slowly dried its wings in the sun.
   A   simple sentence
   B   compound sentence
   C   complex sentence
   D   compound-complex sentence

8. Earlier, the astronauts had put on their spacesuits and strapped themselves down for liftoff.
   A   simple sentence
   B   compound sentence
   C   complex sentence
   D   compound-complex sentence

9. The ranch workers herded the calves into narrow chutes; the veterinarians then vaccinated each animal.
   A   simple sentence
   B   compound sentence
   C   complex sentence
   D   compound-complex sentence

10. Grandma will give whoever learns to play this accordion all her old sheet music; unfortunately, none of the grandchildren are interested.
    A   simple sentence
    B   compound sentence
    C   complex sentence
    D   compound-complex sentence

NAME _____ CLASS _____ DATE _____ SCORE _____

for **CHAPTER 5** pages 154–189

CHAPTER TEST

Agreement: Subject and Verb, Pronoun and Antecedent

DIRECTIONS Read each set of sentences below. Three of the sentences in each set have errors in agreement; one sentence is written correctly. Choose the sentence that is written correctly, with NO ERRORS in agreement.

> **EXAMPLE**
>
> 1. A The sack of apples and grapes are on the front seat of her car.
>   B Neither of the senators are able to answer the reporter's question.
>   C Many of the egrets are going to spend the winter in this marsh.
>   D None of the storm's damage to the houses were serious.
>
> **Answer**

1. A To our surprise, neither the horse's owners nor the jockey are going to accept the trophy.
   B The debate squad was arguing with one another about strategy for the competition.
   C Either the salamander or the frog tadpole are the subject of Lin's paper on amphibians.
   D Which of those books that describe the culture, history, and spiritual life of the Inuit are the one you recommended?

2. A The only member of the pep squad who can do those complicated routines are Billy Joe.
   B After sound waves enter a human ear, it strikes the eardrum and creates vibrations.
   C "Although physics are the most difficult of my courses," said Jane, "I don't mind because I think the equations are fascinating."
   D To my mother's dismay, a swarm of grasshoppers is eating all the corn in her vegetable garden.

3. A Louise says she don't need to study for that quiz because she has read Maya Angelou's story several times.
   B "Yes, *Driving Miss Daisy* is my favorite film of all those I have seen," admitted Evan.
   C Do you think that the statues on Easter Island are one of those mysteries that is unsolvable?
   D American author Flannery O'Connor's characters are remarkable because of its physical deformity or mental instability.

4. A Unfortunately, neither the guide nor my father took their binoculars on the fishing trip.
   B Using contractions, the largest jellyfish ejects jets of water and moves their body upward.
   C Almost everybody who lives on the island of Hawaii is aware it was created by volcanoes.
   D The architect, building engineer, and construction supervisor held his breath as the client inspected the blueprints for the first time.

5. A "I'm afraid that just a few of our staff has decided to attend the meeting," said the manager.
   B Only two dozen of the ninety candles on my great-grandmother's birthday cake was blown out.
   C "*Dust Tracks on a Road*, Zora Neale Hurston's autobiography, are as fascinating as the novels we've read this semester," said Jennifer.
   D Eighty percent of all students in the sophomore class agree that the parking lot should be a recycling collection center on Wednesday evenings.

CHAPTER 5 | Agreement

9

6.
- **A** One of the best recipes in that *Specialties of Mexico* cookbook are sweet tamales, which are filled with fruit.
- **B** Despite the high wind, neither the fronds nor the coconut has fallen from the palm tree.
- **C** Is Jamie's mother, aunt, and sister all physicians in different types of medicine?
- **D** The baseball team have chosen to travel to the playoffs by bus instead of in cars.

7.
- **A** All who are interested in going on to the observatory to learn about stars should raise his or her hand.
- **B** "Well, does anyone in this marching band know how to tune their instrument properly?" asked the conductor.
- **C** Either Lois or Chan are going to be on the committee that will investigate how to make the library collection more up-to-date.
- **D** Of all the artists in our class, Hector is the one painter who is always determined to do his best.

8.
- **A** "Where is my trail mix, my dehydrated food, and my sunscreen?" asked Juanita on the first day of our camping trip.
- **B** Sky blue, soft yellow, and white is the colors in my grandmother's needlepoint pillows.
- **C** From down here on the ground, I am unable to tell whether the spider monkey or the woolly monkey are making that unusual sound.
- **D** Running swiftly over the snow with its huge feet, the hungry lynx pursued the rabbit.

9.
- **A** Several members of the Olympic track team have spent most of their lives preparing for this moment.
- **B** "I'm sure that someone at these tables know which animals use their horns as weapons," repeated our biology teacher.
- **C** To our amazement, we learned that many creatures, such as the arctic fox, is able to change dark fur to white for winter camouflage.
- **D** Have any of the special order of fabric, upholstery thread, and fancy trim arrived yet?

10.
- **A** Even though the football team has not practiced for the two days before the big game, the players doesn't seem nervous.
- **B** Some mollusks, such as the clam, are bivalves; in other words, they have two shells of approximately the same size.
- **C** The acoustics in the concert hall, even though it was built in the nineteenth century, is impressive.
- **D** The contrast between traditional American Indian values and modern-day life in "The Man to Send Rain Clouds" by Leslie Marmon Silko are the subject of Tyrone's essay.

| NAME | CLASS | DATE | SCORE |

for **CHAPTER 6** pages 190–215   **CHAPTER TEST**

Using Pronouns Correctly: Nominative, Objective, and Possessive Case; Clear Reference

DIRECTIONS Read each set of sentences below. Three of the sentences in each set have errors in the use of pronouns; one sentence is written correctly. Choose the sentence that is written correctly, with NO ERRORS in the use of pronouns.

EXAMPLE

1. **A** Caroline and he researched the positions of Aztec pyramids.
   B This song about the class trip is by Thomas, Harold, or she.
   C To our delight, Mom showed us photos of the new puppy and they.
   D Do Kendra and him know that a fish cannot move its tongue?

   Answer

---

1. **A** Bill Cosby is an actor whom is as popular with older generations as he is with younger ones.
   B On the nature program, we saw the lioness carry her male cub from one hiding place to another, which would give he and the other cubs more protection.
   C Mai, George, Alex, and me have requested that the library purchase another encyclopedia on CD-ROM.
   D As a surprise for our mother, Susie and I dusted the bookshelves, cleaned the bathrooms, and made dinner before she came home.

2. **A** It was I who claimed that Bessie Smith is the greatest female blues singer of all time.
   B The sophomore student-council representative is him.
   C Is the herpetologist who specializes in African cobras him or her?
   D It may have been them who played the practical joke on everyone in our science class.

3. **A** Eduardo gave samba lessons to Jerry and she.
   B Between you and I, when Beth shows her new skateboard to Christopher, he will want one just like it.
   C Our science teacher showed Paul and they how Neanderthals and Cro-Magnons are different and pointed out the areas where fossils of each have been found.
   D For him and us, it's important to do volunteer work at the local homeless shelter.

4. **A** The news about the recent discovery of sauropod dinosaur fossils in West Texas thrilled the scientists and us.
   B The graphic-arts experts, him and her, gave a presentation about silk-screen printing to the school art classes.
   C As the judges conferred, the finalists of the speech contest were narrowed to two people, he and she.
   D My grandmother gave her Tiffany lamp, which was decorated with dazzling and colorful dragonflies, to my brother and she as a wedding present.

CHAPTER 6 | Using Pronouns Correctly   11

for CHAPTER 6 pages 190–215 continued

CHAPTER TEST

5. **A** Morgan is the only student in our woodshop class whom knows how to create furniture designs by using the new computer program.
   B Whom could have known that Barbara Jordan, who was a United States representative, is La Toya's source of inspiration and role model?
   C The pharaoh who ordered that those pyramids, tombs, and roads be built was he.
   D Whomever knows the importance of radiation from the sun, please raise your hand.

6. **A** The county-fair judge awarded Bert and me second-place ribbons.
   B Her uncle, a criminal-law attorney, told we members of the debate squad that in the courtroom, charisma can be as important as expertise.
   C In the article in our local paper, it identified the initiators of the water-conservation program, Jane and he.
   D Us sophomores are going to take a field trip to the National Museum of American Art, the National Museum of American History, and the National Air and Space Museum in Washington, D.C.

7. **A** When my parents announced we were going to Miami Beach, no one was as happy as me.
   B Do you and Alissa play tennis doubles more frequently than they?
   C Dan can sing any of the solos his voice teacher, Mr. Gibson, can sing, but not as well as him.
   D Although Mark and Mary are twins, Mary is five minutes older than him.

8. **A** Mrs. Hanson handed silk to Leah to place on the cutting board before she began unfolding the dress's paper pattern.
   B Dad gave Mario his copy of the periodic table before helping us study for the chemistry quiz.
   C When Eliza performed a perfect dive, Wendy cheered for her.
   D Mr. Saunders left Mr. Pedersen's business so that he could take a job that did not require so much travel and so that he could spend time with his family.

9. **A** Raoul is fascinated by owls, which are nocturnal birds of prey; that might explain why he wants to become an ornithologist.
   B According to our minister, there will be a bake sale and silent auction at our church this Sunday, which should be fun.
   C Jonah saw Monica doing volunteer work at the nursing home where his great-grandfather lives, which he thought was very nice.
   D The important role of molds, bacteria, and other agents of decay is the subject of the Web site that we created in my environmental science class.

10. **A** My father is the first person whom danced with the team mascot on the football field after we won the championship.
    B The woman whom he appointed to chair the committee to preserve historical buildings will hold a press conference today.
    C Some people whom are born in the United States have dual citizenship if their parents are citizens of foreign countries.
    D To who should I submit my article about the native seed program at the Wildflower Research Center?

| NAME | CLASS | DATE | SCORE |

for **CHAPTER 7** pages 216–255

CHAPTER TEST

Using Verbs Correctly: Principal Parts, Tense, Voice, Mood

DIRECTIONS Read each set of sentences below. Three of the sentences in each set have errors in the use of verbs; one sentence is written correctly. Choose the sentence that is written correctly, with NO ERRORS in the use of verbs.

EXAMPLE

1. A Watch the clown who leap through the paper hoop.
   B The female kangaroo is carrying a thumb-sized baby in her pouch.
   C After she has opened the gift from her secret pal, Alexandra smiled with pleasure.
   D Hannah is studying hard because she is learned anesthesiology.

   Answer

---

1. A A frog's sticky tongue shoots out as fast as a party whistle unfurls when you blew in it.
   B While I was shopping at the seafood market, I saw oysters, lobsters, crabs, clams, and mussels.
   C Did you know that vertebrates never are having more than two pairs of limbs?
   D For the second event, the triathlete, after swimming a mile in Town Lake, will have jumped on her bike to cycle twenty-eight miles.

2. A Last week, that dog's highly developed sense of smell help it follow a scent trail several days old.
   B To produce tapestries, weavers follow full-size patterns known as cartoons.
   C An important source of protein in the Japanese diet is fish, which can be salted and broiled, prepare raw, or fry in a batter.
   D Lungfish are a unique type of primitive bony fish that had breathed with organs similar to lungs as well as with gills.

3. A Elaine must learn how to make tortillas and other basic Mexican fare before she can take the gourmet Mexican-cuisine course.
   B The farmer had rang the dinner bell for ten minutes before all the workers came in from the field.
   C In addition to memorizing twenty German vocabulary words, Harvey read three chapters of the novel he is studying in English class.
   D Those mosques and minarets look beautiful, didn't they?

4. A The eggplant and zucchini seedlings were planted by my brother yesterday.
   B Although the old mine was searched for months, the geologist found no indication of diamonds.
   C In response to my question, the Langston Hughes poem was read by our literature teacher.
   D The hummingbirds have discovered the bright red hibiscus flowers.

5. A Fossils can be formed by several processes, including carbonization and mummification.
   B The moving parts of clocks and watches are simple, and they are easily repair if you are meticulous.
   C Old records, audiotapes, and videotapes all can be damage by heat.
   D Hydroelectric plants are often build in mountainous areas because of the abundance of falling water; power of the falling water is transformed into electricity.

CHAPTER 7 | Using Verbs Correctly 13

for CHAPTER 7 pages 216–255 *continued* **CHAPTER TEST**

6. A   The toad is laying her jelly-covered eggs, which are called spawn.
   B   That book laying on the table is the grammar book that my great-great-grandfather studied in the early 1900s.
   C   When Juanita lied down her ball of yarn, the cat happily pounced on it.
   D   Please lie the shrimp in the sink so that I can clean them for dinner.

7. A   The hawk set on her large nest of twigs and grass for thirty-two days.
   B   That snapshot of Joel's quartet at the El Paso performance has been setting on top of the TV for weeks.
   C   After eating four large watermelon slices in the contest, Amy set down for a few minutes.
   D   Slobbering and wagging his tail, our Dalmatian set his beloved chew toy at my feet.

8. A   After nibbling on the tomato leaf, the caterpillar rose its head and seemed to stare at us.
   B   Devonne's little brother was frightened because he thought the tyrannosaurus skeleton was raising on its hind legs.
   C   We were happy to learn that the sophomore car wash rose three hundred dollars for the fall dance.
   D   The tide is rising early tomorrow, so we should leave before dawn to go clam digging.

9. A   The dragonfly, which is knowed for its beautiful wings, can fly more than fifty miles an hour.
   B   The monkey swinged from tree to tree in the jungle.
   C   Cheeping loudly, the sparrow stir up quite a commotion while it took a dust bath.
   D   Hector's father has given him a new radio for his car because Hector made the honor roll.

10. A   I was told by my brother that the Web site described historical sites in New Hampshire, Maine, Vermont, and Massachusetts.
    B   "The dodo," said my grandmother, "was a flightless bird that lived on the island of Mauritius."
    C   Osteoarthritis is a disease that occurred when a joint wears out.
    D   The great blue heron spread its long wings and rises into the air.

| NAME | CLASS | DATE | SCORE |

for CHAPTER 8 *pages 256–279*   **CHAPTER TEST**

Using Modifiers Correctly: Forms, Comparison, and Placement

DIRECTIONS Read each set of sentences below. Three of the sentences in each set have errors in the use of modifiers; one sentence is written correctly. Choose the sentence that is written correctly, with NO ERRORS in the use of modifiers.

> **EXAMPLE**
>
> 1. A The colt frolicked in the most largest meadow, rolling in the lush, green grass.
>   B The shell of the largest scallop is beginning to open.
>   C Luisa stood brief to acknowledge the ovation she received for her speech.
>   D A very colorfully place mat showing a bright summer scene was on her table.
>
> **Answer**

1. A Even though my grandmother asked for an honest opinion, I could not admit that her perfume smelled badly.
   B Because of my fair coloring, deep colors such as blue, green, and purple look badly on me; lighter shades look better.
   C Crabs often run sideways on the tips of their legs, and they move less slowly than you would expect.
   D Walk slow and quiet through the woods if you want to see the animals that live there.

2. A After watching the octopus snatch an unsuspecting crab and inject poison into its shell, I did not feel good and asked to be excused.
   B The new hard drive worked well, so Nathan installed several new programs on his computer.
   C To her disappointment but not her surprise, the inexpensive guitar sounded badly.
   D He feels badly that he caused his parents so much disappointment.

3. A In order to stay healthy, you should eat the freshest fruits and vegetables that are available.
   B We are proud that the sophomore cheerleaders can shout more louder than either the junior or the senior squads.
   C Because pythons can swallow large prey whole, they may digest their victims more slow than most other snakes do.
   D Between the Russian and the Japanese figure skaters, which one performed her spin the most quickly?

4. A In my opinion, the state of Texas is more bigger than you can imagine.
   B Organic gardeners believe that it is best to introduce ladybugs to a garden to eat aphids than to use chemicals to kill such pests.
   C Which of the two books is least expensive—the one of nursery-rhymes or the collection of commercial campaigns?
   D In orchestra today, we decided that Midori plays better than any other young violinist.

5. A When we were playing basketball, I realized that my sister's jump shots were better than my father.
   B Grandmother Ramirez prefers her own tortilla chips to the supermarket.
   C Because Janine's father is an agent for musicians, Janine is more knowledgeable about current music than anyone in our class.
   D Elsa has traveled to more states than any other person in my neighborhood.

CHAPTER 8 | Using Modifiers Correctly   15

for CHAPTER 8 pages 256–279 continued **CHAPTER TEST**

6. A Giggling excitedly, my cousin retrieved her gift from under the Christmas tree wrapped in red tissue.
   B The scientist examined microscopic animals and plants floating in water on the slide.
   C Shouting and bounding across the soccer field, the team's enthusiasm was obvious.
   D My mother carefully removed paint from the old dresser using a rag dipped in citrus oil.

7. A The artist showed us the statue of a gazelle and a cheetah sculpted in clay.
   B I gave the diagram of the brain to my friend on which I had written notes.
   C While learning how to tango, a muscle in Kris's calf became sore.
   D Worried that he was going to be late, Bob's scowl covered his entire face.

8. A While camping in the wilderness, trash should be carried out in your backpack.
   B To understand the importance of the Dead Sea Scrolls, their complex history should be read.
   C Running a brush through her hair, the curls shone in the light.
   D After reading chapter 3, Ann knows there are thousands of bacteria on human skin.

9. A We were real excited when the presidential candidates held a debate in our town.
   B The grand prize, a trip to San Francisco, was real; we were afraid it was not genuine.
   C Despite his initial nervousness, Herschel played his trumpet solo real well.
   D I want to tell you something real important.

10. A Determined, the goal was just inches away from the quarterback.
    B The convertible was being repaired by the automobile mechanic with an oil leak.
    C Dreaming about the future, I allowed my thoughts to wander from the lab experiment.
    D The wolf gave the rabbit to her hungry cubs that she had caught and killed.

| NAME | CLASS | DATE | SCORE |

for **CHAPTER 9** pages 280–309

CHAPTER TEST

A Glossary of Usage: Common Usage Problems

DIRECTIONS Read each set of sentences below. Three of the sentences in each set have errors in standard, formal usage; one sentence is written correctly. Choose the sentence that is written correctly, with NO ERRORS in standard, formal usage.

EXAMPLE

1. A A lot of people will be coming to my brother David's bar mitzvah in June.
   B Is there a explanation for why some scorpions are deadly and others harmless?
   C Each of the trainers taught an elephant to raise its trunk on command.
   D Jonathan ain't going to football practice today.

   Answer

---

1. A Accept for Minnie, no one in our health science class can describe the complete path blood takes from the heart through the body.
   B Is it true that this here crocodile seized the young deer and disappeared rapidly under the water?
   C Frowning with concentration, Pablo solved every geometry problem except the last one.
   D If you had been paying attention to where you were walking, you would not have tripped over that there curb.

2. A We thought the chameleon was effected by the color of the leaf, but the sign on the exhibit noted that chameleons change color because of variations in their environment or because of reactions such as fear.
   B Almost anything—including interest rates, political elections, and settlements in lawsuits—can affect the stock market.
   C To our disappointment, it all ready was time to leave the exhibit of paintings by the Mexican artist Frida Kahlo.
   D The water-polo players are already to leave the swimming pool and take a shower.

3. A Being as she loves flowers, my grandmother decided to cultivate orchids as a hobby.
   B Because she made a remarkably accurate model of a section of porous rock that is a reservoir for fossil fuel, Esther won the science prize for sophomores.
   C Is anybody beside you going to try out for the part of Caesar in the school play?
   D This modem is busted, so we're going to call different stores and find a new one at a good price.

4. A Even many historical linguists can't barely understand these Egyptian hieroglyphics.
   B We watched her golden hamster cram the pieces of fruits and vegetables into its cheeks and then put the food in the corner of the cage.
   C Marie looked in the refrigerator for lettuce to put on her sandwich, but she didn't find none.
   D "Its always fun," said my sister, "to stare at clouds and imagine what they resemble."

CHAPTER 9 | A Glossary of Usage   17

for CHAPTER 9 pages 280–309 continued   **CHAPTER TEST**

5. A   Although he has read a half-dozen books about the Galápagos Islands, Alan can't hardly imagine ever getting to see its giant tortoises and swimming iguanas.
    B   "There isn't no reason to be afraid of rattlesnakes, as long as you're careful," said the ranger in Rocky Mountain National Park.
    C   Because our town has grown so much, the city must hire more policemen and firemen.
    D   Any artist who wants to exhibit work at the June art show should allow the committee to review his or her portfolio.

6. A   Josephine Baker could of lived the life of a typical popular entertainer, but she chose to enrich her life by adopting children of many nationalities.
    B   Would you rather read Gwendolyn Brooks's poetry then Emily Dickinson's?
    C   The male peacock, with its colorful tail feathers, is more spectacular than the male turkey.
    D   If you had known you were going to volunteer at the hospital this winter, you should of gotten a flu shot.

7. A   According to organic gardeners, marigolds are just one of many plants that harmlessly keep pests out of vegetable gardens.
    B   Who's muddy boots are these?
    C   Do you know whose planning to get a job at the factory this summer?
    D   Is that the dog who chased your cat around the house and up the big pine tree?

8. A   Vikki is going to try and teach me how to make origami animals out of paper.
    B   The seal, barking energetically, lumbered across the flat rock and then jumped off of the edge into the water.
    C   Owls, storks, doves, and eagles are just a few of them birds that have symbolic meaning.
    D   If you try to understand the meaning of every word in that medieval manuscript, you will not succeed.

9. A   Next year, when I am a junior, I am going to study for the SATs, send away for college brochures, and etc.
    B   When you go to the library this afternoon, would you please bring back these books that are due today?
    C   Fifty miles per hour is all the faster this 1940s car can go, despite its recent tuneup.
    D   "I didn't mean to imply that you weren't telling the truth."

10. A   "It was like living in a blast furnace," responded my great-grandmother when asked what life was like before air conditioning was discovered.
    B   Pointing at a map, the lost tourist asked Johnathan where the statue of Paul Revere was at.
    C   I know it is possible to teach a child a second language when the child is very young.
    D   Leave them go; they are already running late.

| NAME | CLASS | DATE | SCORE |

for **CHAPTER 10** pages 310–335

CHAPTER TEST

Capitalization: Standard Uses of Capitalization

DIRECTIONS Read each set of sentences below. Three of the sentences in each set have errors in capitalization; one sentence is written correctly. Choose the sentence that is written correctly, with NO ERRORS in capitalization.

EXAMPLE

1. A Arnold is going to Nuevo Laredo, Mexico, for one week this Spring.
   B The Missouri supreme court will be closed for the holiday.
   C The Rocky Mountains extend from central New Mexico to north Alaska.
   D a spiral galaxy, the Milky Way moves very slowly.

   Answer

---

1. A Yes, my father's favorite football teams are the Pittsburgh Steelers and the San Diego Chargers.
   B On tuesday, the subject of Mrs. Decker's lecture will be pollen and spores.
   C Kenneth is canadian, but his parents are from Scotland and Ireland.
   D The caged crickets in our Environmental Science Class can be quite noisy.

2. A Did you know that Mayor Gimble lives on Rose street?
   B My uncle Ramón is taking a sculpting course at the Local Community College.
   C *A World of Literature* is the title of our anthology, which was edited by Edith Frank.
   D How many years ago did the ice age end, and does it still affect our climate?

3. A A mobile of the different planets hangs in Marla's room; she likes Saturn and Mars the best.
   B During our field trip to the paleontology Museum, we enjoyed the exhibit on dinosaur digs.
   C In her poem about the seasons, Melanie compared Spring to a happy, innocent maiden and Winter to an old, wise man.
   D Can you believe that the brownsville badgers won the Little League pennant this season?

4. A Her Aunt Rosa collects dolls from France, Germany, Italy, and other countries in europe.
   B "When I was a child," said my grandmother, "Dreft™ was the only detergent that we used."
   C Is it true that Lake Baikal in Siberia holds more fresh water than any other lake in the World?
   D The elephant bird, which lived in madagascar more than one thousand years ago, grew up to ten feet tall.

5. A Our neighbor drives a vintage Ford thunderbird that he restored himself.
   B I will take Calculus, Spanish III, World History, Chemistry, and Home Economics next year.
   C "I found these lovely flowers in the blue ridge Mountains," said Mrs. Wallace.
   D For Chinese New Year, my uncle Chan and his friends will dress in a large dragon costume.

6. A While reading an article in *the Beeville beacon*, Daniel found several capitalization errors.
   B My class report focuses on the Countee Cullen poems "Tableau" and "Incident."
   C She plans to write her report on one of two african american writers: Toni Cade Bambara or Alice Walker.
   D Have you read Ernest Hemingway's story "a day's wait"?

CHAPTER 10 | Capitalization

19

for CHAPTER 10 *pages 310–335* continued

CHAPTER TEST

7. A "*Buddhist Temple by Twilight* is the title of my painting," said Mai proudly.
   B Our school's Audiovisual Club is making a documentary called *Highlights Of High School*.
   C When Janet visits New York this summer, she is going to see the play *The Diary of Anne Frank* on broadway.
   D According to Mr. Jamison, we will perform a scene from William Shakespeare's *a Midsummer Night's Dream*.

8. A After English class, I have German II, Chemistry I, and football practice.
   B The television show about prince Rainier of Monaco will be shown at 9:00 p.m.
   C Linda Herrera's father is a marathoner, and he always wears adidas® running shoes.
   D When I was at camp this summer, a counselor taught me how to find the north star and every planet visible to the naked eye.

9. A The Chief consulted with other tribal leaders about how to improve schools on the Reservation.
   B So far, Becky is the only sophomore who has been asked to go to the Senior Prom this spring.
   C Here on Earth, it is sometimes difficult to imagine that astronauts have walked on the Moon.
   D Before uncle Lester takes us to the aviary, we should learn about some of the unusual birds that we will see.

10. A Tonight, my Mother and I are going to watch *Guess Who's Coming To Dinner* on the classic movies channel.
    B At the bird feeder, we saw Cardinals, Blue Jays, and doves.
    C "I like being a sophomore," said Harold, "Because I'm no longer the new kid on the block and I don't have to worry about college entrance exams yet."
    D In 1862 the USS *Monitor* and the USS *Merrimack* fought the first battle between ironclad warships.

NAME _____ CLASS _____ DATE _____ SCORE _____

for CHAPTER 11 *pages 336–365* **CHAPTER TEST**

Punctuation: End Marks and Commas

DIRECTIONS Read each of the following sets of sentences. Three of the sentences in each set have errors in the use of end marks or commas; one sentence is written correctly. Choose the sentence that is written correctly, with NO ERRORS in the use of end marks or commas.

> **EXAMPLE**
>
> 1. **A** Did you know that cardinals like sunflower seeds the best.
>   **B** Carved by glaciers thousands of years ago the green valley was deep and wide.
>   **C** The shell of atmosphere around our planet responsible for the weather is called the troposphere.
>   **D** Jumping to their feet the crowd gave the soloist a standing ovation.
>
> **Answer**

1. **A** The woolly mammoth, which looked like a hairy elephant, once roamed the earth
   B Are you aware that wood is made of dead plant cells?
   C Gabriella, please don't practice the drums after 10:00 P.M. on weeknights?
   D My goodness. I can almost see that bean sprout growing before my eyes.

2. **A** While brainstorming solutions to the geometry problem, Ryan drew a triangle rectangle, and octagon.
   B "I don't mean to disillusion you," said Mrs. Yang, "but many flowers' aroma and beauty have a purpose—to attract pollinators."
   C The delicate ornate, wrought-iron staircase was the most unusual feature of their home.
   D Yes I'm aware that birds, which have scales on their legs, probably evolved from reptiles.

3. **A** The red, yellow, and orange bands of the rainbow were easiest to see.
   B In areas with high altitudes, such as the Swiss Alps air pressure is low and oxygen is scarce.
   C Ricardo will you be a volunteer for the "Walk Miles in My Shoes" march this Saturday?
   D During a growing season bulbs store food for the shoots that will grow from them.

4. **A** Before baking bread, Alan cleans the counter, and measures all the ingredients.
   B When she explored the CD-ROM's contents, Jenna found detailed information about American Indian burial customs.
   C Well, do you believe his statement that the idea for this colorful energetic painting came to him in a dream?
   D Stopped by the boulder the bulldozer shuddered and then quickly backed up?

5. **A** Some termites, for example, build enormous mounds that can be twenty feet high.
   B The proper embouchure or mouth position, is needed to play any of the wind instruments, such as the flute, saxophone, trumpet, or tuba.
   C Flexing its body and pumping its fins the catfish struggled against the current.
   D Inside the box on top of the refrigerator there is an old, rusty key.

CHAPTER 11 | Punctuation 21

for CHAPTER 11 pages 336–365 continued   CHAPTER TEST

6. **A** Is Josephine Arturo M.D. the most experienced ear, nose, and throat doctor at the clinic?
   B Yes, it's true that African Americans fought on both sides during the Civil War.
   C On June 15 2003 we will move to Nicaragua for a year because my father will teach at a university there.
   D The lizards called flying dragons, can glide through the air by extending folds of skin that look like wings.

7. **A** Do you agree Ahmed, that spiders can be described as architects that design with silk?
   B Squinting through his telescope the astronomer found what he hoped was a new star.
   C My stepmother, who is going to be our softball coach, played varsity softball in college.
   D According to our computer science teacher the school should purchase surge protectors so that electrical "spikes" don't harm the computers.

8. **A** The thick, strong shells of turtles protect them from many predators.
   B Delighted the shouting children ran to hiding places while their grandmother counted to one hundred.
   C On Wednesday, Alan Saunders Jr. will give a free seminar about the best surfing beaches in North America.
   D Sea cucumbers may look harmless but actually these animals have sharp spines deep within their skin.

9. **A** Fascinated, Amanda wanted to run her fingers over the ancient, rock carving, but she remembered that touching the petroglyphs is not allowed.
   B Inside the cage the toucan gobbled the pieces of fruit we had given it.
   C Compared to some other animals human beings have a poor sense of smell; however, we can still distinguish between many different odors.
   D Under the mattress in the master bedroom Grandma's heirloom jewelry is stored in a manila envelope.

10. **A** The lines on that iris are like roads, that point toward its center.
   B Remember, Wendy, that Grandfather will arrive on Tuesday, May 4.
   C Well if you made an A in biology, you probably will do well in chemistry, too.
   D Drought and overgrazing for instance are threatening the grasslands around the Sahara in Africa.

NAME _____ CLASS _____ DATE _____ SCORE _____

for CHAPTER 12 pages 366–381   **CHAPTER TEST**

Punctuation: Semicolons and Colons

DIRECTIONS Read each set of sentences below. Three of the sentences in each set have errors in the use of semicolons or colons; one sentence is written correctly. Choose the sentence that is written correctly, with NO ERRORS in the use of semicolons or colons.

EXAMPLE

1. A   In a magnetic compass, the needle is a bar magnet; and the needle points north along one of the earth's magnetic-field lines.
   B   Paul will: sweep the garage, trim the bushes, and mow the yard.
   C   In October the tree's leaves turned red and began to fall off; by January all of its branches were bare.
   D   The colors in that rug are: pink, purple, blue, and gold.

Answer

---

1. A   I'm going to watch a documentary about Carl Lewis, the Olympic track star; I will also read a book about him.
   B   Roses usually grow best in rich, loamy soil, however, hybrid roses will tolerate sandy or gravelly soils.
   C   Yes, you can make diamonds: but they are very expensive to produce, and as gems they would cost more than natural diamonds.
   D   On Wednesday, Mr. Jones described how waves are formed; and I will never look at the sea the same way again.

2. A   Tyrone has seen sand dunes not only at the beach but also in the desert, however, he has never been in a sandstorm.
   B   Volcanoes exist all over our planet's surface, in fact, they even appear on the ocean floor.
   C   I am looking forward to baby-sitting for the Smiths Friday night; moreover, I hope to baby-sit all day Saturday.
   D   Grandfather has already seen the aurora borealis, or northern lights, in person, he probably won't be interested in that television program.

3. A   Not all dinosaurs grew enormously large; one kind was only about the size of a chicken.
   B   Eye color depends on the parents' genes, for example; the gene for brown eyes is dominant over the gene for blue eyes.
   C   To our amazement, the redwood tree towered dozens; indeed, hundreds of feet above the forest floor.
   D   Plants come in many sizes and shapes consider; for example, single-celled algae and huge oak trees.

4. A   Mara carefully examined the plastic model of the human body and; moreover, identified the location of kidneys for the first time.
   B   "Combining ammonia and bleach creates toxic fumes," said our chemistry teacher; and he warned us to be careful when using household cleaners.
   C   Sea horses have long, strong tails; as a result, these fish are able to cling to seaweed that moves a great deal.
   D   The shape of an animal's teeth reveals much about its diet, for instance, herbivores, or plant eaters, have molars designed to grind plants.

CHAPTER 12 | Punctuation   23

for CHAPTER 12 pages 366–381 continued   **CHAPTER TEST**

5. **A** Javier went to the Cinco de Mayo celebration with Pete, Brad, and me; Sue went with Paulina, Eduardo, and Annie.
   B Please be prepared for a quiz on Monday, April 5, Wednesday, April 24, and Tuesday, May 1.
   C His sister is an expert in foundations, cement, and tiles, and her father is knowledgeable about plaster, roofs, and wood floors.
   D The runner from the strawberry plant has; therefore, made several new plants.

6. **A** Jennifer is interested in: the temples in India, the pyramids in Egypt, and the statues on Easter Island.
   B Pecking with its beak, the chick cracked the shell open, instantly, the hen focused on her new offspring.
   C In Los Angeles, California, we visited several excellent museums: the Getty Center, the Los Angeles County Museum of Art, and the Museum of Contemporary Art.
   D While on vacation, my family has stayed in: hotels, motels, tents, and trailers.

7. **A** At 2 00 P.M. on Saturday, my stepmother's investment club will meet at our house.
   B If you are feeling discouraged, you might try reading Psalm 23: 1–4.
   C We will have these speakers in class on Tuesday; Mayor Lin, Father Baird, and Professor Watson.
   D Plunging its beak into the feeder; the hummingbird withdrew a drop of the bright red sugar water.

8. **A** At the botanical gardens, we examined carnivorous plants such as; venus' flytraps and pitcher plants.
   B Her brother's wheelchair is equipped with: a laptop computer, a book bag, and a cellular telephone.
   C If you learn these Spanish vocabulary words: you will be ready for the quiz.
   D Guadalupe and her friends have been assigned the following tasks for the sophomore dance: decorating the gym, setting up tables, and making punch.

9. **A** Oak trees have a wide range of habitat and can be found in Iowa City, Iowa; Rochester, New York; and Boston, Massachusetts.
   B To make the salsa, Raoul chopped the tomatoes, cilantro, and onions, and I pressed the garlic, squeezed the lemons, and minced the peppers.
   C Proteins contain carbon, hydrogen, nitrogen, and oxygen, some also contain iron, phosphorus, and sulfur.
   D The woodpecker; however, uses its tail as a brace.

10. **A** Every day at 12 00 noon, the bells in the church tower play "Nearer My God to Thee."
   B At the amusement park we rode on: the carousel, the roller coaster, and the bumper cars.
   C Animals defend themselves in these ways: stinging, pinching, fleeing, disguising, and biting.
   D "Some physicists," he said, "are trying to invent a theory that will; moreover, explain everything in the universe."

| NAME | CLASS | DATE | SCORE |

for CHAPTER 13 *pages 382–399* **CHAPTER TEST**

Punctuation: Italics, Quotation Marks, and Ellipsis Points

DIRECTIONS Read each set of sentences below. Three of the sentences in each set use italics or quotation marks incorrectly; one sentence is written correctly. Choose the sentence that is written correctly, with NO ERRORS in the use of italics or quotation marks.

> **EXAMPLE**
>
> 1. A "Cranes," which was written by Hwang Sun-won, is Lisa's favorite story.
>   B "Please watch," said Mr. Percy, "As the butterfly lays her eggs on the leaf."
>   C Have you ever read "Franny and Zooey," a novel by J. D. Salinger?
>   D "I just wrote a haiku that I've titled *Evening Star*," said Catherine.
>
> **Answer**

1. A "Are these scarves on sale"? asked Meredith.
   B "Muddy Road" is a Zen parable in our world literature textbook.
   C "Believe it or not, Franz Kafka's story 'The Metamorphosis' is about a man who wakes up as an insect"!
   D Louella read Arthur Miller's play "Death of a Salesman" while on summer vacation.

2. A "The Train from Rhodesia," a short story by the South African writer Nadine Gordimer, is about invisible barriers between people.
   B "We will be reading Maya Angelou's autobiography 'I Know Why the Caged Bird Sings' this month," said my English teacher.
   C "Look at my painting," Alexandra said proudly, "which is called 'Bear-shaped Clouds.'"
   D My little sister's best-loved bedtime book is "The Cat in the Hat."

3. A "Interestingly enough" said Joe, the behavior of those dogs—nipping at and chasing sheep—is similar to that of their ancestor the wolf."
   B "We are all made of carbon-based molecules," wrote Bonita in her winning science essay.
   C "Although Dr. Martin Luther King, Jr., is probably the most famous U.S. civil rights leader, many others worked hard for social change in the 1950s and 1960s" said our social studies teacher.
   D "If you research President Eisenhower, I'll investigate President Kennedy." offered Patty.

4. A "Yes, it's true that sharks' oily livers help them float because oil is lighter than water", revealed Janie.
   B Could you explain why no one joined the cheerleaders in shouting, "Go, Lions, Go!"?
   C The article concluded, "The Women's League. . . . is looking forward to sponsoring the Special Olympics in our city."
   D "I think the novel 'Lord of the Flies' might be scary for anyone younger than we are," said Bethany.

5. A "I'd prefer that you didn't dot your i's with smiley faces, said Mrs. Carmichael."
   B "The Spanish word for 'sweet' is 'dulce.'"
   C The television show *Father Knows Best* went off the air years ago, but I watch the reruns every week.
   D The song *Blue Suede Shoes* always makes me want to jump up and dance.

CHAPTER 13 | Punctuation   25

6. A Roger admitted, "I finally stopped practicing my trumpet solo when Sarah shouted, "I can't stand this anymore!""

B Many birds, mammals, and even insects migrate, and their journeys can be thousands of miles long," Ron said.

C "To Kill a Mockingbird," a novel by Harper Lee, was made into a movie of the same name.

D If something is "hot," does that mean that it's also "cool"?

7. A Rhonda explained, "The African American writer Zora Neale Hurston traveled throughout Florida, collecting folk tales.

B "In the chapter called *Animals at Work*," he said, "there is a description of leaf-cutter ants and the fungus gardens they build."

C "My brother has started saying the word *groovy* in response to everything I say!" complained Liana.

D Aunt Anne read us excerpts from her poem about hedgehogs, which is titled *Prickly but Perfect*.

8. A "You may think that "Night and Day" is a corny song," said Mom, "but I like every word of it!"

B "My goal.... is to be president of the United States," Leticia finally admitted.

C "Chicken mole," my favorite Mexican dish, contains meat, spices, sesame seeds, and, surprisingly, cocoa.

D The *Queen Mary*, a luxury ship that was launched in the 1930s, took more than four days to cross the Atlantic Ocean.

9. A "Granted, some countries still have a lot of coal," said Mr. Elliot "but this resource is depleted every day."

B "I love you more than the sun and moon," said my mother. "But what about the stars"? asked my little brother.

C "Don't forget your change, sir!" called the cashier.

D Did you read the article *What's New in Fitness?* in today's newspaper?

10. A The guide continued, "These flowers are very rare." "They are found in only two other places on earth."

B "When I "surf" the Internet," I explained to my brother, "I don't actually use a surfboard."

C When the baby says "bah," he means *bird*.

D Do you think that the local museum should buy Henry Robinson's painting 'Mother and Child'?

NAME _____ CLASS _____ DATE _____ SCORE _____

for **CHAPTER 14** pages 400–421

CHAPTER TEST

Punctuation: Apostrophes, Hyphens, Dashes, Parentheses, Brackets

DIRECTIONS Read each set of sentences below. Three of the sentences in each set use apostrophes, hyphens, dashes, parentheses, or brackets incorrectly; one sentence is written correctly. Choose the sentence that is written correctly, with NO ERRORS in the use of punctuation.

EXAMPLE

1. A Helen and Miranda's literature textbooks are on the coffee table.
   B James's mother, Debbie Garnet, is an attorney specializing in tax law.
   C The set designer removed the theater's curtain and then repaired it's fringe.
   D Three-fourths of the sophomores will attend the homecoming game.

   Answer Ⓐ ●Ⓑ Ⓒ Ⓓ

---

1. A On Friday the advanced art class will take a field trip to see Edward Hoppers paintings at the art museum.
   B That millionaires charities range from orphanages to computer-training academies.
   C This children's television show will discuss at least a few of the thousands of different amphibian species.
   D Dana Jones is the leader of our drill team, and Mikki Lan is the captain of their's.

2. A Jasper's dog, a huge Saint Bernard, has been chosen as the basketball team's mascot.
   B Installing a lily pond in the backyard was someone elses' good idea.
   C Teds' report is about macaque monkeys, which have adapted to cold winters in Japan.
   D Hector and Antonio's football jerseys are covered with mud because the field was soaked by rain.

3. A Even though wed tossed wildflower seeds all over our yard, none of them sprouted and grew in the spring.
   B Who's backpack was left in the school's darkroom this weekend?
   C At four o'clock on Saturday, he'll give a presentation on villages in northern Tibet.
   D Its easier to see the hairs on that carnivorous sundew plant if you use a magnifying glass.

4. A Mrs. Junipero says there are too many *he*'s and *she*'s in my writing; she suggests that I occasionally replace these pronouns with names.
   B According to this article, "The (board's) report mentioned that skateboards and roller skates have become a nuisance in the park."
   C Is that book about the evolution of jazz music your's, his, or her's?
   D Heather made straight *A*s on the chemistry tests, so she's not going to do an experiment for extra credit.

5. A Grandma and I canned twenty five quarts of peaches last weekend.
   B Some naturalists think that geeses' triangular flight formation is designed to reduce wind drag for each bird.
   C Charles Dickens's family was poor (it's no surprise that his books often mention money), and Dickens himself went to work at age twelve.
   D The effects of prolonged drought could be devastating. (See page 315 (Chart B) for a projection.)

CHAPTER 14 | Punctuation   27

NAME _____ CLASS _____ DATE _____

for **CHAPTER 14** pages 400–421 continued

CHAPTER TEST

6. **A** A three-fourths majority is necessary before the chess club can make any change to its bylaws.
   B If you add one-half of a cup of plain flour, it will be easier to knead the rye bread dough.
   C That brightly-colored and sequined prom dress is sure to attract attention.
   D On Mondays, Wednesdays, and Fridays next fall, my stepfather will teach a self-motivation course at the local community college.

7. **A** Weary and sore after their long hike through the Austrian and Swiss A-lps, the mountaineers were glad to be home.
   B All twenty-four of the people in my class—it's advanced biology received good grades on the test about vertebrate anatomy.
   C Christopher's job [believe it or not] is to clean insect fossils by using a toothbrush.
   D I was not surprised to learn that every animal and plant on earth, as well as most micro-organisms, requires oxygen to survive.

8. **A** The honeypot ant stores honey in its abdomen and shares the liquid with other ants' when prompted.
   B Is it true that squids and octopuses—both relatives of the cuttlefish—can change the colors and patterns of their bodies?
   C The snow fell constantly for twenty four hours—until it had made three-foot drifts in our front yard.
   D Abraham Lincoln, despite our image of him as a modest and vanity-free man—changed beard styles many times during his life.

9. **A** Mr. Molina knows how to make all my favorite Mexican dishes—*carne asada*, enchiladas, and *camarónes en escabeche.*
   B Leeches—contrary to popular belief—can be beneficial creatures and sometimes are used to reduce swelling in surgery patients.
   C The impala—which roams the lightly wooded areas of Africa, eats fruit, grass, and leaves.
   D Shooting across the sky—the meteor moved too quickly for me to take a photograph.

10. **A** Please sketch a diagram of the muscles in a cat. (you do not need to draw in color)
    B Yes, we are impressed that her grandfather (he's ninety years old) swims every day, even when the lake is icy cold.
    C The Panama Canal, my mother had wanted to see it all her life, stretched before us.
    D Whitney Houston (she is an excellent singer and actress—will give a concert there this weekend.

NAME _____ CLASS _____ DATE _____ SCORE _____

for CHAPTER 15 *pages 422–453* **CHAPTER TEST**

Spelling: Improving Your Spelling

DIRECTIONS Read each set of sentences below. The underlined word is spelled incorrectly in three of the sentences in each set; in one of the sentences, the underlined word is spelled correctly. Choose the sentence in which the underlined word is spelled CORRECTLY.

EXAMPLE

1. A   We percieve only a limited number of colors in the spectrum.
    B   Okay, I conceed that Janine is a better singer than Debby.
    C   Could you estimate the height of that remarkable termite nest?
    D   You'll get no arguement from me; Annette is going to win the championship title.

    Answer   Ⓐ   Ⓑ   ●   Ⓓ

---

1. A   "Is there any difference between bees, wasps, and hornets?" asked my sister.
    B   Did you see that clever advertisment for computers on TV last night?
    C   Plants realy do produce chemicals that discourage predators.
    D   "Please proceed to the exit," said the guide after our tour of the Roman Colosseum.

2. A   A rainbow forms a complete circle; however, we usually can't see more than half of it.
    B   "Unfortunately, I mispelled the word *verbose* during the sophomore class's spelling bee," said Paulette.
    C   That old pickle barrel is useable, even though it has a leak; perhaps we could plant flowers in it.
    D   The livelyness of our Great Dane is matched only by the boundless energy of our German shepherd.

3. A   In the begining, my parents had just the one shoe-repair shop.
    B   Those dragon and snake kites's were handmade by my grandfather.
    C   Look! There are three wild turkies beneath the willow tree!
    D   Melinda and he are digging trenches for the new sprinkler system.

4. A   I'm afraid all I have are seventeen pennys.
    B   The photographer Ansel Adams is famous for his photoes of the wilderness.
    C   On Saturday in the gymnasium, the alumnis of the class of 1995 will hold a reunion brunch.
    D   Is it true that salmon return to the rivers from which they came?

5. A   The members of our book club have many different believes about what constitutes great literature.
    B   Squeaking with excitement, the mouses ran to the crumbs of Swiss cheese.
    C   "You are allowed to use @s in your e-mail addresses, but I would prefer that you not use them in your essays," said Mr. Ashioki.
    D   The editor in chiefs of that new journal on artificial intelligence are my grandparents.

6. A   5,262 species of plants exist on that mountain, according to the team of botanists.
    B   Despite countless hours of rehearsal, the sophomore a cappella singing group placed only 3rd.
    C   This cinder cone is one thousand two hundred fifteen feet above sea level.
    D   Three hundred fourteen penguins are in that island's colony.

CHAPTER 15 | Spelling   29

for CHAPTER 15 pages 422–453 continued   **CHAPTER TEST**

7. A On April Fools' Day, which is celebrated on April <u>1st</u>, twenty sophomores filled the biology lab with balloons.
   B Contrary to our expectation, the rock that contained traces of iron did not <u>effect</u> the magnet.
   C During our vacation, we drove <u>two thousand six hundred forty-two</u> miles across North America.
   D "I was not <u>affected</u> by the cold weather," insisted the marathon runner.

8. A "Of <u>coarse</u> they once were molten lava," said the geologist, pointing at the shiny, black rocks.
   B His sister Rebecca cannot <u>here</u>, but she is an expert in reading lips and signing.
   C Do you know if Tiger Woods has played on this golf <u>course</u>?
   D If we sit <u>hear</u> for an hour or two, perhaps the storm will blow over.

9. A Are <u>their</u> factors besides mineral content that determine a soil's fertility?
   B "Could you please remove the crusts from <u>they're</u> toast?" asked Mother.
   C Bills outstretched, the little pelicans begged <u>their</u> mother for more food.
   D Hydrangea flowers change <u>there</u> color according to the acidity or alkalinity of the earth.

10. A If you go there, be sure <u>too</u> watch the crabs climb up and down the mangrove trees.
    B "<u>To</u> many cooks spoil the broth," said my sister as she led the rest of us out of the kitchen.
    C These <u>two</u> dogs are very active and require vigorous exercise every day.
    D "<u>Whose</u> been sleeping in my bed?" my sister kept demanding after I read her the story of Goldilocks and the three bears.

NAME _____ CLASS _____ DATE _____ SCORE _____

for CHAPTER 16 | *pages 454–487*   **CHAPTER TEST**

Correcting Common Errors: Key Language Skills Review

DIRECTIONS Read each set of sentences below. Three of the sentences in each set have errors in key language skills; one sentence is written correctly. Choose the sentence that is written correctly, with NO ERRORS.

EXAMPLE

1. A Don't Alana or Frank have a video camcorder that we could use?
   B An interesting silver and pink pinstripe running the length of each side of the truck.
   C "Those are your's," she patiently explained for the fourth time to her youngest sister, "and these are mine."
   D Before we knew it, we had passed the exit for Interstate 95 and were on our way to who knows where.

   Answer Ⓐ Ⓑ Ⓒ ●D

---

1. A Everybody who is anybody will be there with their dancing shoes on.
   B None of the events went as we had planned, but we all had a good time anyway.
   C All of us must remember his or her manners when we visit the Senator's office.
   D Anyone with tickets remaining should bring their unsold tickets to the main office by the end of the day.

2. A Have you ever went to Iran, where your parents were born?
   B Because she had never swam in the ocean before, she wasn't ready for the waves to be so strong.
   C Every evening around 5:30 P.M., our cat goes out to the driveway and just sets there, waiting for Mom to come home from work.
   D Ms. Kelly asked Dave for his opinion of Federalists, and he gave it—for twenty minutes until the bell rang.

3. A I've seen a lot of bad, low-budget movies, but this one was the baddest of all.
   B Did you read about that giant fish that they caught in the newspaper?
   C Thinking back on my tiredness today, my mistake was obvious: I should have eaten breakfast.
   D Actually, I enjoy the opera more than anyone else in my family does.

4. A Until the principal approves the nominees, we cannot release the names of anyone who the committee has selected.
   B Ms. Vander and myself will sponsor the campus cleanup campaign.
   C Mr. Wright and us guys usually meet to work on a special project in the shop room after school on Thursdays.
   D You don't need to go to all this trouble just for Justin and me.

5. A These figures don't look too badly; let's review the rest of the spreadsheet.
   B It just don't get no better than this—a cool breeze, a hammock, and a good book.
   C I never thought when we laid the carpet that it would look so good.
   D The reason for the delay is because the principal has to discuss this matter with the school board.

CHAPTER 16 | Correcting Common Errors   31

for **CHAPTER 16** pages 454–487 continued

CHAPTER TEST

6. **A** I am honored to present our sponsor, Mr Ernesto Chin.
   B Although poets in the past immortalized military campaigns in poems like "The Charge of the Light Brigade" modern poets seldom do so.
   C Direct all inquires to Ruff and Ready Software, Forelli Avenue, Torrance, CA 90509.
   D Mao Zedong (His name is also spelled *Mao Tse-tung.*) was the major figure in the formation of the People's Republic of China and the Chinese Communist Party.

7. **A** Sometimes, the line between a language and a dialect is blurred, for instance, the Canadian and Maine variety of French known as *joual* is sometimes labeled a language and other times labeled a dialect.
   B An active figure in the Harlem Renaissance, Alain Locke was a Rhodes scholar; he wrote several books that detailed the artistic achievements of black Americans.
   C This area is off limits to: visitors, unauthorized personnel, and delivery drivers.
   D In the testing area, these items are prohibited, calculators, paper, and books of any kind.

8. **A** You can thank the Hawaiians for the word "ukulele"; the original Hawaiian word refers to a flea jumping.
   B I must have reread the novel "King of the Wind" twenty times.
   C Is it true that the title of your story is "Turtles and Roller Skates?"
   D "Diane always says, 'Call me,' but she's never home," Ravi complained.

9. **A** Known throughout the country as a master of electronic music.
   B When an owner diligently follows the maintenance schedule suggested by the manufacturer.
   C Sacagawea assisted Meriwether Lewis and William Clark on their quest for a Northwest Passage; her ability as a translator was invaluable as the expedition traveled through unfamiliar territory.
   D Computer technology can be helpful and time saving, however, one must maintain a working knowledge of basic mathematical facts in order to use software appropriately.

10. **A** Evidently, the person who's access code was written on the bottom of the mouse pad compromised the whole network.
    B Its easy to see how much Angela loves her horse: She's at the stable every chance she gets.
    C Look at this great photograph of Machu Picchu, that Incan fortress city in Peru.
    D Think carefully before you answer these questions, class.

| NAME | CLASS | DATE | SCORE |

for **CHAPTER 17** page 490

TEST

Writing Complete Sentences

DIRECTIONS Read the passage and select the best answers for the questions that follow. Some parts of the passage need to be rewritten. Some questions are about particular sentences and ask you to identify flaws in sentence structure. Other questions ask you to choose the best correction or revision of a sentence. In making your decisions, follow the conventions of standard written English. After you have chosen your answer, fill in the corresponding circle on your answer sheet.

Questions 1–20 are based on the following passage.

(1) One interesting animal of the American Southwest is the javelina (pronounced "have-a-LEE-na"). (2) Though they appear similar to pigs. (3) Javelinas are members of a completely different biological family. (4) The javelina, the most numerous of the three surviving species of their family, but the smallest in size. (5) An individual weighs between fifty and sixty pounds.

(6) Javelinas from Argentina to Arizona, New Mexico, and Texas. (7) They are social animals, living together in small groups typically numbering six to ten. (8) May have as many as fifty animals.

(9) Javelinas cannot tolerate extremes of heat and cold, so the American Southwest might seem a strange environment for them. (10) Finding suitable places and adapting their behavior. (11) They pack themselves together at night to save heat and find shaded places to spend the day. (12) They are most active at dawn and dusk.

(13) Javelinas eat plants. (14) Stories that they sometimes prey on small birds and mammals have not been proven. (15) Fierce fighters, though. (16) Their razor-sharp teeth and ability to successfully counterattack predators make them dangerous foes for coyotes, mountain lions, and occasional foolish dogs.

(17) In areas of the southwestern United States. (18) Development has reduced the javelina's habitat. (19) The javelinas' food supply, natural trails, and bedding areas are disappearing, people and javelinas meet more frequently. (20) When new residents first encounter their wild neighbors. (21) Later their pleasure turns to dismay if javelinas lack enough space, they destroy gardens and yards. (22) Who feed and water the animals contribute to the problem. (23) Providing them with food and water makes javelinas dependent on people. (24) Wildlife experts that javelinas can coexist with people. (25) Habitat areas for javelinas can be created in areas that have only one house for every ten acres.

(26) Relocation efforts for javelinas have had mixed results. (27) Creating new herds with relocated javelinas is not easy, some entire groups have died. (28) Like many species, may ultimately lose in conflicts with humans.

1. Which sentences in the first paragraph are sentence fragments?
   (A) sentences 1 and 2
   (B) sentences 2 and 3
   (C) sentences 2 and 4
   (D) sentences 3 and 4

2. Why is sentence 6 a sentence fragment?
   (A) It is missing a subject.
   (B) It is missing a verb.
   (C) It is missing both a subject and a verb.
   (D) It is missing a prepositional phrase.

3. Which of the following represents the best revision of sentence 6?
   (A) Javelinas range from Argentina to Arizona, New Mexico, and Texas.
   (B) The range of javelinas will from Argentina to Arizona, New Mexico, and Texas.
   (C) Javelinas can from Argentina to Arizona, New Mexico, and Texas.
   (D) From Argentina to Arizona, New Mexico, and Texas, is the range of javelinas.

GO ON

CHAPTER 17 | Writing Complete Sentences

33

NAME _____ CLASS _____ DATE _____

for CHAPTER 17 page 490 continued

TEST

4. Which of the following represents the best revision of sentence 8?
   - (A) Groups may have as many as fifty animals.
   - (B) May have, in some cases, as many as fifty animals.
   - (C) May have as many as fifty animals in a group of javelinas.
   - (D) Javelinas may have as many as fifty.

5. What is the most serious problem with sentence 10?
   - (A) It expresses a complete thought.
   - (B) It has no verb.
   - (C) It has no subject or verb.
   - (D) It has no subject.

6. Which of the following represents the best revision of sentence 10?
   - (A) Finding suitable places to adapt their behavior.
   - (B) Javelinas find places most suitable and adapting their behavior.
   - (C) Javelinas finding suitable places and adapt their behavior.
   - (D) Finding suitable places and adapting their behavior help javelinas survive.

7. Which of the following is a sentence fragment?
   - (A) sentence 12
   - (B) sentence 13
   - (C) sentence 14
   - (D) sentence 15

8. The fragment you identified in Question 7 lacks
   - (A) a subject
   - (B) a conjunctive adverb
   - (C) a noun
   - (D) a subject and a verb

9. What is the problem with sentence 17?
   - (A) It is a run-on.
   - (B) It is a sentence fragment.
   - (C) It lacks a verb.
   - (D) It lacks a subject.

10. Which of the following represents the best revision of sentences 17–18?
    - (A) In developing areas of the southwestern United States, growth of javelina's habitat.
    - (B) The southwestern United States is growing with the javelina's habitat.
    - (C) In areas of the southwestern United States, development has reduced the javelina's habitat.
    - (D) The javelina's habitat has reduced the growing development of the southwestern United States.

11. What is the most serious problem with sentence 19?
    - (A) It lacks a subject.
    - (B) It lacks a verb.
    - (C) It is a sentence fragment.
    - (D) It is a run-on sentence.

12. Which of the following represents the best revision of sentence 20?
    - (A) When new residents first encounter their wild neighbors, they may be charmed.
    - (B) When first encountering their wild neighbors.
    - (C) When new residents first encounter their wild neighbors, being charming.
    - (D) Javelinas encounter new residents they charm their wild neighbors.

GO ON

for CHAPTER 17 page 490 continued   TEST

13. Which of the following statements best describes sentence 20?
    (A) It lacks a verb.
    (B) It expresses a complete thought.
    (C) It cannot stand alone as a sentence.
    (D) It lacks a subject.

14. What is the most serious problem with sentence 21?
    (A) It is a run-on sentence.
    (B) It is an incomplete thought.
    (C) It is a sentence fragment.
    (D) It has no subject or verb.

15. Which of the following represents the best revision of sentence 22?
    (A) Homeowners who feed and water the animals.
    (B) Homeowners who feed and water the animals contribute to the problem.
    (C) Homeowners who feed and water contribute to the problem.
    (D) Who feed and water the animals homeowners contribute to the problem.

16. Which of the following statements best describes sentence 23?
    (A) It does not express a complete thought.
    (B) It is a sentence fragment.
    (C) It is a complete sentence.
    (D) It is a run-on sentence.

17. Which of the following represents the best revision of sentence 24?
    (A) Wildlife experts claiming that javelinas can coexist with people.
    (B) Wildlife experts that javelinas coexist with people claiming.
    (C) Wildlife experts claim that javelinas can coexist with people.
    (D) Wildlife experts can that javelinas coexist with people.

18. Which of the following represents the best revision of sentence 25?
    (A) Habitat areas for javelinas can be created. In areas with only one house for every ten acres.
    (B) Habitat areas for javelinas can be created in areas with only one house. For every ten acres.
    (C) For javelinas can be created in areas with only one house for every ten acres.
    (D) Habitat areas for javelinas can be created in areas with only one house for every ten acres.

19. Which of the following represents the best revision of sentence 27?
    (A) Creating new herds with relocated javelinas, some entire groups have died.
    (B) Creating new herds with relocated javelinas not being easy because some entire groups have died.
    (C) Creating herds with javelinas is not easy, some entire groups have died.
    (D) Creating new herds with relocated javelinas is not easy; some entire groups have died.

20. What is the best way to correct sentence 28?
    (A) Like many species, will ultimately lose in conflicts with humans.
    (B) Like many species, javelinas may ultimately lose in conflicts with humans.
    (C) Like many species may ultimately losing in conflicts with humans.
    (D) In conflicts with humans like many species, may ultimately lose.

CHAPTER 17 | Writing Complete Sentences

Writing Effective Sentences

for CHAPTER 18 page 502 — **TEST**

DIRECTIONS *Alison has written this report for a science class. As part of a peer writing conference, you are asked to read the report and think about what suggestions you would make. When you finish reading the report, answer the multiple-choice questions that follow.*

Volcanoes: Destructive and Creative

1 We think of volcanoes as destructive. Volcanoes are also creative. Volcanoes played
2 a key role in shaping and changing the earth. They did so long before humans existed.
3 Volcanoes created more than 80 percent of the earth's surface, which was pushed up by
4 the pressure of the earth's core. Gases produced with those eruptions helped create the
5 atmosphere. The gases gave the earth elements essential to life.
6 The word *volcano* comes from *Vulcano*. That is the name of a small island in the
7 Mediterranean Sea. Ancient peoples believed that the lava, smoke, and dust spewing from
8 the island were the work of the god Vulcan. Vulcan was a Roman god. He was a black-
9 smith, and people believed he made thunderbolts for all-powerful Jupiter, and he made
10 weapons for the war-god Mars, and the island was named for him.
11 Volcanoes are mountains, but unlike other mountains, they are not formed by the
12 folding and uplifting of the earth's surface. They rise by the accumulation of their own
13 vented products. A volcano is usually a cone-shaped mountain. The mountain is formed
14 around a vent, or opening, in the earth's surface. The vent connects to the molten rock
15 beneath the earth's surface. Molten rock is lighter than solid rock, and it rises to the surface.
16 It may flow. It may explode. An explosion can shoot gases, rock, and ashes far into the sky.
17 The annihilation of Pompeii in A.D. 79 shows the destruction volcanoes can cause. The
18 environmental damage to forests and wildlife in 1980 also shows the destruction. Mount
19 Vesuvius destroyed the cities of Pompeii and Herculaneum. Mount Saint Helens caused
20 $1.2 billion in damage. Over time, volcanic activity is good for the earth and to help peo-
21 ple. Volcanic materials eventually become fertile soils. Volcanic matter provides construc-
22 tion materials, cleaning and finishing products, and raw materials for chemical and
23 industrial purposes. Heat from volcanic systems can be used for geothermal energy.
24 Scientists do not know everything about how volcanoes work. Continuing research into
25 volcanic eruptions helps us prepare for one of nature's most dramatic forces.

GO ON

NAME _____ CLASS _____ DATE _____

for CHAPTER 18 page 502 continued

TEST

1. What is the **BEST** way to rewrite the first two sentences in line 1? (*"We think . . . also creative."*)
   A. We think of volcanoes as destructive, and volcanoes are also creative.
   B. We think of volcanoes as destructive and creative.
   C. We think of volcanoes as destructive, but they are also creative.
   D. We think volcanoes as destructive when they are also creative.

2. What is the **BEST** change, if any, to make in the sentences in lines 1–2? (*"Volcanoes played . . . humans existed."*)
   F. Volcanoes played a key role in shaping and changing the earth, and they did so long before humans existed.
   G. Long before humans changed the earth, volcanoes played a key role in shaping existence.
   H. Volcanoes played a key role in shaping and changing the earth long before humans existed.
   J. Make no change

3. What is the **BEST** change, if any, to make in the sentences in lines 4–5? (*"Gases produced . . . to life."*)
   A. Gases produced with those eruptions helped create the atmosphere, giving the earth elements essential to life.
   B. Gases produced with those eruptions helped give the earth its essential atmosphere to life.
   C. Gases produced with those eruptions helped create the atmosphere, gases giving elements essential to life.
   D. Make no change

4. What is the **BEST** change, if any, to make in the sentences in lines 6–7? (*"The word . . . Mediterranean Sea."*)
   F. The word *volcano* comes from *Vulcano*; that is the name of a small island in the Mediterranean Sea.
   G. The word *volcano* comes from *Vulcano*, the name of a small island in the Mediterranean Sea.
   H. The name of a small island in the Mediterranean Sea, *Vulcano*, comes from the word *volcano*.
   J. Make no change

5. What is the **BEST** way to rewrite the sentences in lines 7–8? (*"Ancient peoples . . . Roman god."*)
   A. Ancient peoples believed that the lava, smoke, and dust spewing from the island were the work of the god Vulcan, who was a Roman god.
   B. Vulcan was a Roman god, which ancient peoples believed that the lava, smoke, and dust spewing from the island were the work of the god.
   C. Ancient peoples believing that the lava, smoke, and dust spewing from the island were the work of a Roman god who was Vulcan.
   D. Ancient peoples believed that the lava, smoke, and dust spewing from the island were the work of the Roman god Vulcan.

6. Which of the following **BEST** describes the sentence in lines 8–10? (*"He was . . . for him."*)
   F. a simple sentence
   G. a complex sentence
   H. a stringy sentence
   J. a wordy sentence

GO ON

CHAPTER 18 | Writing Effective Sentences

7 What is the BEST way, if any, to rewrite the sentence in lines 11–12? ("*Volcanoes are . . . earth's surface.*")

   A Volcanoes are mountains, but volcanoes are unlike other mountains. Volcanoes are formed by the folding and uplifting of the earth's surface.

   B Volcanoes are mountains, but unlike other mountains. They are not formed by the folding and uplifting of the earth's surface.

   C Volcanoes are mountains, but they are unlike other mountains, and they are not formed by the folding and uplift of the earth's surface.

   D Make no change

8 What is the BEST way, if any, to rewrite the sentences in lines 13–14? ("*A volcano . . . earth's surface.*")

   F A volcano is usually a cone-shaped mountain which forms around a vent, or opening, in the earth's surface.

   G A volcano is usually a cone-shaped mountain, which is around a vent, or opening, in the earth's surface.

   H A volcano is usually a cone-shaped mountain that is a vent, or opening, in the earth's surface.

   J Make no change

9 What is the BEST way, if any, to rewrite the sentences in line 16? ("*It may . . . may explode.*")

   A It may flow and it may explode.

   B It may flow or explode.

   C It may flow, or it may exploding.

   D Make no change

10 What is the BEST way, if any, to rewrite the sentences in lines 17–18? ("*The annihilation . . . can cause.*")

   F The annihilation of Pompeii in A.D. 79 shows the destruction volcanoes can cause; The environmental damage to forests and wildlife in 1980 also does.

   G The annihilation of Pompeii in A.D. 79 shows the destruction volcanoes can cause, and the environmental damage to forests and wildlife in 1980 also shows the potential destruction.

   H The annihilation of Pompeii in A.D. 79 and the environmental damage to forests and wildlife in 1980 show the destruction volcanoes can cause.

   J Make no change

11 Which of the following statements BEST describes the problem with the sentence in lines 20–21? ("*Over time . . . help people.*")

   A It lacks parallel structure.

   B It lacks simple words.

   C It is a sentence fragment.

   D It is a run-on sentence.

12 What is the BEST way, if any, to rewrite the sentences in lines 24–25? ("*Scientists do . . . dramatic forces.*")

   F Scientists do not know everything about how volcanoes work, because continuing research into volcanic eruptions helps us prepare for one of nature's most dramatic forces.

   G Preparing for one of nature's most dramatic forces, scientists do not know everything about how volcanoes work and continuing research into volcanic eruptions help us.

   H Although scientists do not know everything about how volcanoes work, continuing research into volcanic eruptions helps us prepare for one of nature's most dramatic forces.

   J Make no change

NAME _____ CLASS _____ DATE _____ SCORE _____

for **CHAPTER 18** page 502 continued

TEST

DIRECTIONS *Greg has written this report for a music course. As part of a peer writing conference, you are asked to read the report and think about what suggestions you would make. When you finish reading the report, answer the multiple-choice questions that follow.*

The Development of the Piano

1 The piano is a versatile instrument used in everything from classical to rock music.
2 The instrument is also a complex mechanical device. Its complexity is surprising.
3 The piano was actually the solution to a technical problem of early instruments.
4 Harpsichords limited volume. Other early keyboard instruments slowed players down.
5 In order for a string struck by a hammer to sound effectively, the hammer had to
6 rebound instantly. If the hammer were set too close to the string, the hammer bounced
7 back against the string again, especially if struck hard. If it were set too far away the
8 action was slow. The hammers had to move quickly. They had to stay in control. The
9 hammer action had to be set close enough to allow the musician to play rapidly, yet
10 keep the hammers from wild bouncing that turned music to mush. The instrument had
11 to be touch-sensitive. It had to be touch sensitive to keep each note true.
12 Bartolomeo Cristofori came up with the answer around 1700. He devised a system
13 of levers called an escapement that allowed hammers to fly free to the strings, to
14 rebound, and resetting. The escapement stopped the hammers in time for the next
15 notes. The instrument was originally called a harpsichord with soft and loud. The
16 instrument solved the problem. The Italian words *piano e forte* gradually shortened to
17 the name for the instrument known as the piano. The words were for "soft and loud."
18 Vast, sophisticated and refined enhancements and alterations have made the piano a
19 superior instrument since then and have made it one of the most complex mechanical
20 musical instruments played today.

13 What is the **BEST** way to combine the sentences in line 2? ("*The instrument . . . surprising.*")

  A The instrument is also a complex mechanical device, its complexity is surprising.

  B The instrument is also a complex mechanical device which is surprising.

  C The instrument is also a surprisingly complex mechanical device.

  D The instrument, also mechanical device of surprising complexity.

14 What is the **BEST** way to combine the sentences in line 4? ("*Harpsichords limited . . . players down.*")

  F Harpsichords limited volume; other early keyboard instruments slowed players down.

  G Harpsichords and other early keyboard instruments limiting volume and slowing players down.

  H Other early keyboard instruments slowed players down. Because harpsichords limited volume.

  J Limited volume slowed players down on harpsichords and other early keyboard instruments.

CHAPTER 18 | Writing Effective Sentences

for CHAPTER 18 page 502 continued   TEST

15 All the sentences in line 8 begin the same way. Which of the following would be the **BEST** way to combine two sentences to add variety to the sentence beginnings? ("*The hammers ... in control.*")

   A To stay in control, the hammers had to move quickly.
   B The hammers had to quickly stay in control.
   C Quickly, the hammers had to move and stay in control.
   D The hammers had to move quickly to stay in control.

16 The sentences in lines 10–11 begin the same way. Which of the following would be the **BEST** way to combine sentences to add variety to the sentence beginnings? ("*The instrument ... note true.*")

   F The instrument had to be touch-sensitive and keep each note true.
   G To keep each note true, the instrument had to produce different volume levels.
   H The instrument had to be touch-sensitive because it had to keep each note true.
   J It had to be touch-sensitive, it also had to keep each note true.

17 What is the **BEST** change, if any, to make in the sentence in lines 12–14? ("*He devised ... and resetting.*")

   A He devised a system of levers called an escapement allowing hammers flying free to the strings, to rebound, and reset.
   B He devised a system of levers called an escapement that allowed hammers to fly free to the strings, to rebound, and to reset.
   C He devised a system of levers called an escapement that allowed hammers to fly free to the strings, rebounding, and then to reset.
   D Make no change

18 What is the **BEST** change, if any, to make in the sentences in lines 15–16? ("*The instrument was ... the problem.*")

   F The instrument was originally called a harpsichord with soft and loud and it solved the problem.
   G The instrument solved the problem and it was originally called a harpsichord with soft and loud.
   H The instrument, which was originally called a harpsichord with soft and loud, solved the problem.
   J Make no change

19 What is the **BEST** way to combine the sentences in lines 16–17? ("*The Italian ... as the piano.*")

   A For the name of the instrument known as the piano, the Italian words gradually shortened for "soft and loud," *piano e forte*.
   B The Italian words for "soft and loud," *piano e forte*, gradually shortened to the name for the instrument known as the piano.
   C The Italian words for "soft and loud", *piano e forte*, gradually shortened, the name for the instrument known as the piano.
   D Make no change

20 What is the **BEST** change, if any, to make in the sentence in lines 18–20? ("*Vast sophisticated ... played today.*")

   F Refinements and sophisticated changes since then have made the piano a superior instrument and have made it one of the most complex mechanical musical instruments played today.
   G Refinements and changes in the piano since then have made it one of the most complex mechanical instruments played today.
   H Vast, sophisticated, and refined enhancements have made the piano a superior instrument and one of the most complex mechanical musical instruments played today.
   J Make no change

Understanding Paragraphs and Compositions

for CHAPTER 19 page 520

TEST

DIRECTIONS In the passages that follow, certain words and phrases are underlined and numbered. In the right-hand column, you will find alternatives for each underlined part. You are to choose the one that best expresses the idea, makes the statement appropriate for standard written English, or is worded most consistently with the style and tone of the passage as a whole. If you think the original version is best, choose "NO CHANGE."

You will also find questions about a section of the passage or about the passage as a whole. These questions may refer to an underlined portion of the passage or to a specific paragraph.

For each question, choose the alternative you consider best and blacken the corresponding circle on your answer sheet. Read each passage through once before you begin to answer the questions that accompany it. You cannot determine most answers without reading several sentences beyond the question. Be sure that you have read far enough ahead each time you choose an alternative.

Passage I

[1]

To own a restaurant is to be a restaurateur. A career as a restaurateur is a respected and challenging one that requires common sense, energy, and a variety of management and personal skills.

[2]

Successful restaurateurs possess two distinct sets of skills. First are the skills and knowledge that are invisible to the public, such as accounting, food preparation, and general business principles. A restaurateur must be willing to put in long hours. Second are the visible skills. These include interpersonal and communication skills. Both sets of skills are essential to the success of a restaurateur.

[3]

Accounting is high on the list of necessary, but invisible, skills. Restaurant ownership is a risky business; three-quarters of new restaurants fail in the first seven months, usually due to poor cash flow management. Beyond financial management, a restaurateur has to be able to oversee or manage all aspects of the establishment, including cooking and service. The owner has to have enough knowledge to be

1. Which of the following is true about the thesis statement?
   A. It simply states the topic.
   B. It has a topic and a main idea.
   C. It is not very specific.
   D. It simply states the main idea.

2. Paragraph 2, a body paragraph, contains
   F. a thesis statement and supporting details
   G. an introduction and transitional phrases
   H. an implied main idea and a concluding sentence
   J. a topic sentence, supporting sentences, and a clincher

3. What sentence does not belong in paragraph 2?
   A. Successful restaurateurs possess two distinct sets of skills.
   B. A restaurateur must be willing to put in long hours.
   C. Second are the visible skills.
   D. Both sets of skills are essential to the success of a restaurateur.

4. In paragraph 3 what kind of elaboration is used to tell why accounting is a necessary skill?
   F. a personal experience
   G. an expert opinion
   H. a reason
   J. an example

GO ON

CHAPTER 19 | Understanding Paragraphs and Compositions

41

able to hire people who are expert cooks and waiters. A restaurateur needs to be able to rely on key personnel.

[4]

Restaurateurs put their interpersonal skills to work each day as they give instructions to and work alongside their staff. As employers, they can be demanding yet respectful. They can recognize their employees' strengths and weaknesses and still challenge them to improve performance. If an owner has one set of rules for how to treat staff and another for how to treat customers, the owner may seem false to customers. The tone that a restaurateur sets with the staff will be apparent in the overall mood of the restaurant. If the restaurateur shows respect for the staff, respect from staff and customers alike will be returned.

[5]

Restaurateurs put it all on the line every time they greet a customer. Making customers feel special or making their dining experience special in some way is vital to a restaurant's success. Basic politeness goes a long way in helping people feel welcome. Remembering people's names is another way to make customers feel as though they are appreciated. The bottom line is that diners have to feel comfortable about both the food and the way they are treated.

[6]

Do you think you have what it takes? Are you willing to work eighty hours a week? Can you read a spreadsheet? Do you enjoy being around people and helping them feel at ease? The challenges of being a restaurateur are balanced by the rewards of running a successful, respected eating establishment.

5. What purpose does paragraph 4 serve in the composition?
   A. It elaborates on the second set of skills mentioned in paragraph 2.
   B. It explains a step in the process of becoming a restaurateur.
   C. It describes each subtopic of the thesis statement in paragraph 1.
   D. It introduces and explains the writer's point of view.

6. In what order are the details in paragraph 4 presented?
   F. in spatial order
   G. in logical order
   H. in chronological order
   J. in order of importance

7. What is the implied main idea to which the sentences in paragraph 4 relate?
   A. Restaurateurs have to cater to their employees.
   B. Restaurateurs must hold high standards for their employees.
   C. Restaurateurs should make sure that their customers are happy.
   D. Restaurateurs must use excellent communication and people skills.

8. F. NO CHANGE
   G. Finally, restaurateurs put it all on the line.
   H. Instead, restaurateurs put it all on the line.
   J. As a result, restaurateurs put it all on the line.

9. What does the writer accomplish with the series of questions in the concluding paragraph?
   A. The writer catches the reader's interest.
   B. The writer adds further background information.
   C. The writer ties together the main points.
   D. The writer elaborates on the paragraph's topic sentence.

Passage II

[1]

Have you ever driven a remote-controlled car? I know of a neat one. It's called a rover. It weighs twenty-three pounds and is about two feet long. This little rover speeds along at just two feet per minute. However, it has a $265 million price tag.

[2]

To offset the speed and the price, the rover has extra appeal because it is 119 million miles away. Your radio signals will take about ten minutes to reach the vehicle. Each time you set the rover in motion, you help it collect valuable data about the surface of Mars.

[3]

The rover is the result of a joint venture between the National Aeronautics and Space Administration (NASA) and the Jet Propulsion Laboratory (JPL) in Pasadena, California. The rover's mission represents NASA's renewed determination to launch orbiters, landers, and rovers to explore Mars. As a result of NASA's research, scientists are becoming convinced that there is frozen water on Mars.

[4]

The history of our ideas about life on Mars goes back at least to the late 1800's. An Italian astronomer observed and sketched what he called *canali*, natural channels or artificial canals, on the surface of Mars. Percival Lowell, a wealthy amateur astronomer, chose to believe that these canals were made, not just formed. He wanted to view these canals himself. Lowell built his own observatory and spent years mapping the canals, which he thought were the Martians' last attempt to save their final traces of water.

10. What technique does the writer use in the introduction?
    F. The writer asks an engaging question.
    G. The writer shares a personal anecdote.
    H. The writer states a simple thesis.
    J. The writer uses a startling fact.

11. What provides coherence between paragraph 1 and paragraph 2?
    A. The use of *it is* in the second line of paragraph 2 to refer to the rover.
    B. The use of *your* in the third line of paragraph 2.
    C. The reference to speed and price, which were mentioned in paragraph 1.
    D. The use of measurements in both paragraphs.

12. In what way does the introduction of this composition follow a "funnel" format?
    F. It moves from specific information to general information.
    G. It circles from one point to the next, connecting all the points.
    H. It moves from general information to a more specific statement.
    J. It provides background information.

13. What purpose does paragraph 3 serve within the body of the composition?
    A. It supports the writer's opinion.
    B. It gives background information.
    C. It shows a shift in time.
    D. It explains a certain step in a process.

14. F. NO CHANGE
    G. Also, Lowell built his own observatory
    H. Consequently, Lowell built his own observatory
    J. Instead, Lowell built his own observatory

[5]

Years of speculation and science fiction stories bring us up to the 1960's and 1970's. NASA developed a series of missions known by the name Mariner. Early on, flyby missions gave us stark, black-and-white images of the planet. Then, in the early 1970's, a Mariner orbiter sent back images of what looked like flood channels formed by a river. In 1976 two landers, *Viking 1* and *Viking 2*, tested soil samples but found no signs of life. It wasn't until seventeen years later that NASA visited Mars again. This time the visitor was the Mars *Observer*. Scientists acquired hardly any data from the probe before it malfunctioned and stopped transmitting.

[6]

Out of that failure was born *Pathfinder*, the little rover's mother ship. Padded by airbags, *Pathfinder* bounced to the Martian surface on July 4, 1997. For more than two months, the rover, named *Sojourner*, followed commands and explored the planet. Scientists spied more evidence of water. One piece of evidence is that there is sand on Mars. On Earth, sand is formed when water breaks down rock.

[7]

On September 27, *Pathfinder* stopped transmitting. JPL officials assume that extreme temperatures caused some sort of damage. Without *Pathfinder*, *Sojourner* cannot send or receive signals. Before it fell silent, *Sojourner* and the lander sent back more than 17,000 images of the Martian surface. Despite its price tag, this little remote-controlled car has carried us a step further in our quest for knowledge about the mysterious planet Mars.

15. Why isn't the information in paragraphs 4 and 5 presented in one paragraph?
   A. The paragraphs have different topics.
   B. Paragraph 5 begins a new argument.
   C. The final sentence of paragraph 4 wraps up the discussion of the history.
   D. Paragraph 5 shows a shift in time.

16. In what order are the ideas in paragraph 5 presented?
   F. order of importance
   G. spatial order
   H. logical order
   J. chronological order

17. In paragraph 6, which type of direct reference establishes coherence with paragraph 5?
   A. pronouns
   B. repeated words
   C. rewording of ideas
   D. transitional words

18. In paragraph 6, what type of information is used to elaborate on the evidence about water on Mars?
   F. an expert opinion
   G. a fact
   H. a statistic
   J. a personal experience

19. What is the main idea that gives the composition unity?
   A. NASA spent millions on the rover.
   B. The rover collected valuable information about Mars.
   C. The rover discovered water on Mars.
   D. NASA has trouble learning about Mars.

20. What technique does the writer use in the conclusion?
   F. a restatement of the thesis
   G. a summary of the main point
   H. a call for specific action
   J. a reference to the introduction

Reading Workshop: Personal Reflection

DIRECTIONS Read the passage. Then read each question about the passage. Decide which is the best answer to the question. Then mark the space for the answer you have chosen.

What's in a Name?

I have always loved birds—those amazing creatures of flight and song. As a child, I kept a log in which I described in loopy handwriting the sight of a soaring red-tailed hawk and the flutelike song of the western meadowlark. Years later, when I took an ornithology course, I was certain I wanted to become a biologist. However, my interest waned immediately when I discovered that my textbook was not full of glossy pictures of beautiful birds but long lists of unfamiliar, scientific names. I halfheartedly learned that one magnificent bird of prey is called *Buteo jamaicensis*, and the fluting trill that woke me on summer mornings belongs to the *Sturnella neglecta*. I almost closed the book on birds until I realized there was another fascinating level to the study of birds—the stories and humor hidden in their scientific names.

The history behind scientific naming is simple and logical. In order to share information and prevent confusion, scientists from around the world use a universal method of identifying animals. The first rules for assigning scientific names were established in the 1700s. Since that time, they have been refined into an international code. Scientists follow the guidelines when naming newly discovered creatures. Each name must uniquely identify the animal and be easy to pronounce. Latinized words with grammatically correct Latin spellings are preferred. Once names are assigned, they can never be changed by individuals. Since 1930, an explanation of the name's meaning has been required.

The world of scientific naming became clearer to me once I realized that the names are a lot like human names. Each animal has a first, middle, and last name, as well as nicknames. In addition, the scientific names often provide clues to birth dates, locations, and relatives.

I also learned that scientific names are creative and fun. They often demonstrate a sophisticated sense of humor and history. For example, the *Antheraea polyphemus* moth is named for a mythical creature, while a *Zeus* is a powerful fish, and the *Draculoides bramstokeri* is a spider. There is a beetle named *Agra vation*, and a *Verae peculya* is a wasp. Geography is covered, too. The *Panama canalia* and the *Australia* are both wasps. The people who named these creatures managed both to provide unique, descriptive names and to make biology students smile for years to come.

From *A* (*Aaadonta*, a snail) to *Z* (*Zyzzyzus*, a hydroid or plantlike sea creature), acronyms, anagrams, palindromes, oxymorons, and puns, as well as funny sounding words are used to name creatures. With this in mind, I approached my ornithology textbook with renewed interest. I could see a wealth of knowledge in the lists of names, which unfurled before me like an ancient scroll full of intriguing tales. The lists so inspired me that I decided not to become a scientist, and I became a teacher instead. Now I spend my days teaching young people about the stories behind the names of science.

GO ON

for CHAPTER 20 page 558 continued

TEST

1 Which word best describes the author's feelings upon first seeing lists of scientific names for birds?
 A hopeful
 B interested
 C bewildered
 D frightened

2 The phrase "my interest waned" best describes the author's —
 F deep involvement in studying different kinds of birds
 G actions while observing the colors and songs of birds
 H reaction to looking at pictures of birds
 J reaction to memorizing scientific names of birds

3 Which is the most likely reason that rules are required for assigning scientific names?
 A to communicate clearly in a universal language
 B to follow strict scientific procedures in research
 C to prevent more than one discovery of the same bird
 D to maintain correct spellings of Latin names

4 The words *fluting trill* are an example of —
 F a metaphor
 G factual detail
 H sensory detail
 J personification

5 According to the passage, what is the most logical reason that scientific names of animals are not changed?
 A Changing names is unscientific.
 B To have many names for an animal would be confusing.
 C Changing names is against the naming code.
 D First choices are best.

6 Which of these is a figurative detail?
 F . . . to make biology students smile for years to come.
 G . . . unfurled before me like an ancient scroll . . .
 H . . . glossy pictures of beautiful birds . . .
 J . . . song of the western meadowlark.

7 After learning about naming birds, the author found that the ornithology textbook became —
 A colorful
 B ordinary
 C ponderous
 D fascinating

8 Which of the following is the best example of a factual detail in the passage?
 F I described in loopy handwriting the sight of a soaring red-tailed hawk . . .
 G The history behind scientific naming is simple and logical.
 H The first rules for assigning scientific names were established in the 1700s.
 J With this in mind, I approached my ornithology textbook with renewed interest.

9 The significance of the author's experience is best revealed by the —
 A half hearted study of birds
 B attempts to keep a bird log
 C decision to become a teacher
 D study of ancient bird art

10 Which event changed the author's attitude about birds' scientific names?
 F creating lists of birds with similar calls
 G working for the ornithology teacher during the summer
 H studying a history book
 J discovering that birds' scientific names are like people's names

46 ELEMENTS OF LANGUAGE | Fourth Course | *Chapter Tests in Standardized Test Formats*

Writing Workshop: Personal Reflection

for CHAPTER 20 page 568

TEST

DIRECTIONS This passage is an early draft of a student essay. Some parts of the passage need to be rewritten. Read the passage and select the best answers for the questions that follow. Some questions are about particular sentences or parts of sentences and ask you to improve sentence structure and word choice. Other questions refer to parts of the essay or the entire essay and ask you to consider organization and development. In making your decisions, follow the conventions of standard written English. After you have chosen your answer, fill in the corresponding oval on your answer sheet.

(1) I stood in the recording studio alone. (2) "Who would hear my tape?" I wondered. (3) "Would my audience be a panel of judges or one person? (4) Would my unknown audience know how difficult it is to play the viola?" (5) These and other questions was running endlessly though my head like a tape-loop.

(6) I was making a tape for an application to music school. (7) I wanted to become a concert violist, and the recording was the first step. (8) I placed the bow on the strings to practice. (9) I remembered why I switched from the violin to focus on the viola. (10) Larger than a violin, the viola has a deeper, richer sound that makes me think of autumn, with its cool air and bright leaves.

(11) The taped audition was like a qualifying round in a contest. (12) I had played in front of audiences for recitals and auditions, but this was different. (13) I knew I could retape my performance. (14) I did not feel more confident. (15) In fact, I actually wished that I had someone to give me feedback. (16) I closed my eyes and imagined my viola teacher listening and nodding as she did when she was pleased.

(17) I started to play, and it felt like any other performance. (18) Later, when I listened to the tape, all my flaws seemed magnified. (19) My immediate instinct was to try again. (20) Instead, I listened again and heard the musical expression that I had practiced. (21) If I corrected some missed notes, I might lose the musical quality. (22) I sent the recording to the judges and tried to forget about the whole thing.

(23) The results of my taped audition came in the mail. (24) I were accepted to the school. (25) I felt relieved and excited. (26) I began to plan for the future. (27) Now, each time I hear the tape, I cringe less at my mistakes. (28) I will probably have to audition without an audience again, but this tape will always be important to me. (29) I won't perform that sonata again. (30) It was the first time I truly understood myself as a musician.

1. In relation to the passage as a whole, what is the function of the first paragraph?

   (A) To summarize and clearly state the significance of the experience.
   (B) To grab the reader's attention and hint at the meaning of the experience.
   (C) To connect the experience with other common experiences.
   (D) To order the events in a way that will be clear to the reader.

GO ON

CHAPTER 20 | Reflecting on Experiences | Writing Workshop 47

for **CHAPTER 20** page 568 continued TEST

2. Which of the following represents the best revision of sentence 5?

   (A) These questions was running endlessly though my head like a tape-loop.
   (B) This question were running endlessly though my head like a tape-loop.
   (C) These and other questions were running endlessly though my head like a tape-loop.
   (D) Other questions was running endlessly though my head like a tape-loop.

3. Which of the following is the best way to combine sentences 8 and 9 (reproduced below)?

   I placed the bow on the strings to practice. I remembered why I switched from the violin to focus on the viola.

   (A) Placing the bow on the strings to practice, I remembered why I had switched from the violin to focus on the viola.
   (B) I placed the bow on the strings to practice, remembered why I switched from the violin to focus on the viola.
   (C) Placing the bow on the strings to practice and I remembered why I switched from the violin to focus on the viola.
   (D) As I placed the bow on the strings to practice, I was remembering why I switched from the violin to focus on the viola.

4. What is the function of the second paragraph?

   (A) To state the meaning of the experience.
   (B) To get the reader's interest.
   (C) To elaborate on the thoughts and feelings of other people in the narrative.
   (D) To elaborate on the thoughts and feelings of the writer.

5. Which of the following is the best way to combine sentences 13 and 14 (reproduced below)?

   I knew I could retape my performance. I did not feel more confident.

   (A) My performance I could retape and I did not feel more confident.
   (B) I knew I could retape my performance which I did not feel more confident.
   (C) Not feeling more confident, I knew I could retape my performance.
   (D) Knowing I could retape my performance, I still did not feel more confident.

6. What is the function of sentences 17–22?

   (A) To include dialogue.
   (B) To explain a series of events or actions.
   (C) To elaborate on existing details.
   (D) To elaborate on details about people.

for **CHAPTER 20** page 568 continued

TEST

7. Which sentence in the last paragraph is unnecessary to the experience?

   (A) sentence 23
   (B) sentence 27
   (C) sentence 28
   (D) sentence 29

8. Which of the following represents the best revision of sentence 24?

   (A) If I were accepted to the school.
   (B) I was surprised that I were accepted to the school.
   (C) I was accepted to the school.
   (D) I would be accepted to the school.

9. Which of the following represents the best combination of sentences 25–26 (reproduced below)?

   I felt relieved and excited. I began to plan for the future.

   (A) Beginning to plan for the future, I felt relieved and excited.
   (B) For the future, I felt relieved and excited to plan.
   (C) Relieved and excited, I began to plan for the future.
   (D) Planning, I felt relieved and excited for the future.

10. In relation to the passage as a whole, what is the function of sentence 30?

    (A) To add new thoughts and feelings.
    (B) To state the significance of the experience.
    (C) To restate the basic events of the experience.
    (D) To provide factual details.

CHAPTER 20 | Reflecting on Experiences | Writing Workshop

49

Reading Workshop: Comparison-Contrast Article

DIRECTIONS Read the title and the selection. Read each question, and choose the best answer. Mark the space for the answer you have chosen.

Two Sides of the Brain: Both Have Something to Offer

Physically, the two hemispheres, or sides, of the brain seem to be mirror duplicates of each other. Despite this apparent symmetry, however, scientific research has shown that the brain's two hemispheres are functionally different. The left hemisphere controls the right half of the body, and the right hemisphere controls the left half. Nerves connect the opposing sides in the spinal column and in the corpus callosum, where the two sides of the brain meet.

Split-brain research is a fairly recent area of study. It began with discoveries made while observing patients who had lost either left-side or right-side brain function. For example, it was noted that left-hemisphere damage adversely affected speech and language competence. This led to the conclusion that these skills are located in the left side of the brain. Such discoveries have supplied a foundation for further study. Advances in research tools and techniques are allowing scientists to pinpoint which parts of the brain are responsible for certain activities and responses. By recording brain waves and monitoring blood flow in each hemisphere of the brain, researchers can correlate these aspects of brain activity with various kinds of mental performance. These observations have enhanced our understanding of the complexities of human intelligence.

Generally speaking, creativity and intuition are associated with the right side of the brain; abilities of a more analytical or logical nature are located in the left hemisphere. Functions of the right side also include spatial perception and pattern recognition. As mentioned, the left side is the primary center of language.

It is important, however, not to oversimplify these distinctions. Such thinking can lead to stereotyping. A "left-brained" person might thus be classified as a whiz at math but dull and unimaginative; a "right-brained" thinker might be considered creative but unfocused and illogical. Such classifications do not accurately represent the whole picture.

A more wholistic view tells us that while the hemispheres' specific functions may differ, these functions interrelate in such a way as to enhance each other's effectiveness. For instance, the left side of the brain uses an analytical, focused approach to find a specific answer to a problem. Simultaneously, the right brain uses a broader approach to examine the problem, seeking out complexities and subtleties that the left brain might miss. These combined functions enlighten the thinker, allowing recognition of the solution. Even within a particular skill area, both sides have something to offer. Music is a good example of this. While the ability known as perfect pitch is located in the left side of the brain, the activity of listening to music seems to take place on the right side.

Numerous theories about intelligence have been proposed, many of which have been based primarily on analysis of mental performance. Advances in biological testing of the brain are playing an important role as intelligence theories continue to evolve. The biological differences between the left and right sides of the brain are distinct, but neither hemisphere is at its best without the help of the other.

NAME _____ CLASS _____ DATE _____

for **CHAPTER 21** page 596 continued
TEST

1 In paragraph 1, which word provides a clue that this is a comparison-contrast article?
A scientific
B however
C controls
D sides

2 The first discoveries in the field of split-brain research were made studying —
A adults with interesting brain-wave patterns
B young children who were learning language
C musicians who played instruments
D patients who had suffered brain damage

3 In this article, the subjects are grouped —
A haphazardly
B together
C separately
D in sequence

4 According to this passage, right-brain and left-brain functions are —
A exactly identical
B unconnected
C insignificant
D distinct but related

5 What is the *main* idea of paragraph 3?
A Human intelligence can be measured in split-brain studies.
B Each side of the brain is associated with unique functions.
C Using the left side of the brain allows you to function creatively.
D Brain research is advancing because of recent technological developments.

6 Characterizing someone as "left-brained" probably is —
A an oversimplification
B sympathetic concern
C an accurate classification
D a wholistic concept

7 The focus of paragraph 5 is on —
A a single point
B a single subject
C paired points
D multiple subjects

8 Identifying left- and right-brain functions provides a foundation for the study of —
A emotional illness
B mathematical concepts
C human intelligence
D athletic training

9 Which method is used to compare and contrast in this article?
A context clues
B block
C point-by-point
D repeated points

10 What is the *main* idea of this passage?
A Scientists are finally discovering ways to study human experience.
B The brain's two sides perform different functions but operate together for mental effectiveness.
C Musicians use one side of the brain to appreciate music and the other side to sing.
D In the human brain, the left and right sides are duplicates with exactly the same functions.

CHAPTER 21 | Exploring Comparisons and Contrasts | Reading Workshop

for **CHAPTER 21** page 606

TEST

Writing Workshop: Comparison-Contrast Essay

DIRECTIONS *As part of a peer writing conference, you are asked to read the following comparison-contrast essay and think about what suggestions you would make. When you finish reading the essay, answer the multiple-choice questions that follow.*

The People's Choice

1   Elections give citizens a chance to sit in public office. In the United States, voting
2   includes a preliminary step called a primary, or "preliminary" election. A primary election
3   occurs first in time, coming before the general election. In brief, a primary election is prepa-
4   ration for a general election.
5   Formal primary elections are unique to the United States. The election event that is most
6   close in function to a United States primary is in Australia where the Australian Labour
7   Party has a "preselection ballot." Primaries are also used for state and local offices. The
8   process receives very intense media attention during the presidential election. A few states
9   still hold caucuses, or meetings, to select presidential candidates. In most states, however,
10   presidential primaries are formal elections held to determine how state delegates will vote
11   at the party conventions. This is called an indirect primary because the delegates represent
12   the majority of votes in the election; individual votes do not determine selection of the can-
13   didate. In an open primary, voters can choose a candidate from any party. This is not true
14   in a closed primary.
15   General elections are held in many parts of the world. In the United States, a bigger
16   election takes place after the candidates are chosen by a primary vote. At this time, voters
17   have the option of crossing party lines and voting for the candidates of their choice. In a
18   presidential election, their votes are not direct. Each state has a number of "electors," corre-
19   sponding to its number of senators and representatives in Congress. These electors make
20   up the Electoral College, as defined by the U.S. Constitution. Electors, using the popular
21   votes of their states' voters, really elect the President and Vice President.
22   Primaries and general elections have different rules and processes. The opportunity to
23   make choices about public officials is an essential part of the democratic process.

GO ON

NAME _____ CLASS _____ DATE _____

for **CHAPTER 21** page 606 continued

TEST

1. What is the **BEST** way to rewrite the first sentence in line 1? ("*Elections give . . . public office.*")
   - A Citizens should find chances to express their opinions about government.
   - B Elections give citizens opportunities to vote for public officials.
   - C When citizens vote in elections, they are able to have more power and privileges.
   - D Elections give citizens the chance to choose public officials sometimes.

2. What sentence should be added in line 2 to define a subject in the essay?
   - F The primary determines the candidates in the general election.
   - G A primary is held much earlier than the general election.
   - H A primary is the election when the candidates begin their public jobs.
   - J The primary is the last chance to vote.

3. What is the **BEST** change, if any, to make in the sentence in lines 5–7? ("*The election . . . 'preselection ballot'.*")
   - A Change *close* to **closer**
   - B Delete *close*
   - C Change *most close* to **closest**
   - D Make no change

4. What is the **BEST** change, if any, to make in lines 7–8? ("*The process . . . presidential election.*")
   - F Delete *media*
   - G Change *intense* to **furious**
   - H Change *very* to **particularly**
   - J Make no change

5. What is the **BEST** way to rewrite the sentence in lines 13–14? ("*This is . . . closed primary.*")
   - A This is not true in a closed primary.
   - B In a closed primary, voters must choose from their affiliated party's candidates.
   - C Voters in a closed primary must vote differently for the candidates.
   - D Closed primaries are different.

6. Which is the **BEST** change, if any, to make in the sentence in lines 15–16? ("*In the . . . primary vote.*")
   - F Change *a bigger* to **another**
   - G Change *a bigger* to **the general**
   - H Change *primary* to **smaller**
   - J Make no change

7. Which transition should be added to the beginning of the sentence in lines 17–18? ("*In a . . . not direct.*")
   - A Furthermore,
   - B For example,
   - C But,
   - D Still,

8. Which is the BEST change, if any, to make in the sentence in lines 20–21? ("*Electors, using . . . Vice President.*")
   - F Change *states'* to **own**
   - B Delete *really*
   - H Change *really* to **actually**
   - J Make no change

9. What words should be added to the end of the sentence in line 22 to link the conclusion with the thesis? ("*Primaries and . . . and processes.*")
   - A and most people choose to participate.
   - B but both offer voters chances to make and state their political choices.
   - C but they do have the element of choice.
   - D and they both allow voters to have their say.

10. What is the **BEST** change, if any, to make in lines 22–23? ("*The opportunity . . . democratic process.*")
    - F Change *an* to **a very**
    - G Insert **extremely** before *essential*
    - H Change *essential* to **interesting**
    - J Make no change

CHAPTER 21 | Exploring Comparisons and Contrasts | Writing Workshop   53

Reading Workshop: Cause-and-Effect Article

DIRECTIONS Read the passage. Then read each question that follows the passage. Decide which is the best answer to each question. Mark the letter for that answer.

Opportunity

In ancient Greece, girls participated in sports only in limited ways and were not even permitted to watch the Olympic games. In several cultures throughout history, females have been discouraged from becoming athletes. They often had few opportunities to compete in sports while they were young.

Many United States' high schools had sports programs for females, but funding to develop well-run and interesting competitions was limited. Even if a high school female showed athletic ability, she had little opportunity to win an athletic scholarship or have a professional sports career. Athletic opportunities for females were so few that many did not dare dream of pursuing their interest in sports.

In spite of limited opportunities, some female athletes excelled. During the 1930s and 40s, "Babe" Didrikson impressed the public with her superstar athletic abilities in multiple sports, especially track and golf. The All-American Girls Professional Baseball League attracted nearly ten million baseball fans during the 1940s and 50s. In 1967, Kathryn Switzer became the first woman to enter the Boston Marathon.

In 1972, the sports picture for females finally changed in the United States when Congress passed the Federal Educational Amendments, including Title IX. Title IX opened up new possibilities by stating that no person in the United States shall, on the basis of sex, be excluded from participation in, be denied the benefits of, or be subjected to discrimination under any education program or activity receiving Federal financial assistance." The stage was set for females to develop their athletic potential.

When Title IX became law in 1972, about 800,000 females participated in high school sports. By 1984, nearly twice as many were involved in school sports. In 1996, almost 2.5 million females participated in school athletic events. Clearly, once athletic opportunities were offered, females were eager to play.

It was not always easy for school administrators to implement Title IX. It took many lawsuits and many determined females to open up such sports as volleyball, soccer, tennis, basketball, golf, and softball to widespread participation. Their determination paid off.

Basketball has become a particular favorite of high school females, and women's professional basketball has benefited from those who excelled on school courts. One outstanding example is Lynette Woodard. A few short years after Congress passed Title IX, Woodard played on the championship basketball team of Wichita North High School. In 1985, she signed with the Harlem Globetrotters.

For many people, Title IX has become synonymous with opportunity. As females' participation in school sports has evolved, so have the numbers of athletic scholarships. As females have continued to participate and compete throughout their high school and college years, professional opportunities for them have also increased.

Perhaps some of the females who are playing high school softball and baseball will play in a professional league—maybe even in the majors. Title IX holds out the promise of success in sports to all athletically inclined females.

GO ON

| NAME | CLASS | DATE |

for CHAPTER 22 page 632 continued

TEST

1. From this article, you can infer that opportunities for females in sports —
   A will continue to expand
   B have peaked
   C were unwarranted
   D have followed a steady progression

2. Prior to 1972, a female who showed athletic promise could expect —
   F a great deal of recognition
   G few or no chances to play
   H an athletic scholarship
   J a professional career

3. Why did female participation in sports increase?
   A greater public interest in basketball
   B establishment of more baseball leagues
   C the Boston Marathon
   D Title IX

4. Before 1972, athletic opportunities for females were limited because —
   F there had been no successful women athletes
   G females did not want to participate in sports
   H sports for females were not a major part of school athletic programs
   J only certain sports were acceptable to females

5. Which of these is the thesis of this passage?
   A Opening professional sports to women has been an easy transition.
   B Babe Didrikson led the campaign for more participation in female sports.
   C Sports opportunities for females increased because of the Educational Amendments.
   D Funding for high school female sports programs was too low before the 1950s.

6. In this article, the structural focus is mostly —
   F causal chain
   G causes
   H effects
   J composite

7. Which of these is a causative verb in the passage?
   A impressed
   B benefited
   C signed
   D holds

8. The next to the last paragraph demonstrates a pattern that —
   F traces a causal chain
   G emphasizes causes
   H emphasizes effects
   J shows no cause-and-effect relationship

9. From this article, you can tell that the increase in professional female sports —
   A causes increased funding for school programs for female athletes
   B contributes to a decline in scholarships
   C is an effect of more basketball facilities
   D is a result of increased participation in school athletic programs for females

10. What does the title of this article represent?
    F a cause
    G an effect
    H neither a cause nor an effect
    J both a cause and an effect

CHAPTER 22 | Examining Causes and Effects | Reading Workshop   55

NAME _____ CLASS _____ DATE _____ SCORE _____

for CHAPTER 22 page 644

TEST

Writing Workshop: Cause-and-Effect Explanatio

DIRECTIONS *The following essay was written by a student for English class. Read the passage (which may contain some errors) and answer the questions that follow. Be sure to fill in the bubble next to the answer you choose. Mark like this ○ not like this ⊘. You may look back at the passage as you answer the questions.*

Start Your Engines

1   Energy is the body's most basic need. When you eat, you are supplying your body with
2   the fuel for energy. Energy is essential to all activities. Thus, eating the right proportions
3   of different kinds of foods is very important. The USDA's MyPyramid tells people what
4   to eat.

5   The pyramid guides people to eat a variety of foods from five basic categories, called
6   the major food groups. The purpose of the pyramid is to help people eat better every
7   day, by following its recommendations. People will get the nutrients they need while
8   maintaining a healthy weight.

9   The body is constantly breaking down and building up its components. Unlike a car,
10 maintenance must be done by the body while it fuels the mechanical work of its mus-
11 cles. The number of calories needed to do this each day depends upon how much ener-
12 gy an individual's body uses. (A Calorie is the unit of measurement for energy
13 available in foods.) This is where the pyramid comes in, because not all nutrients are
14 converted into energy in the same way.

15 The food groups represent basic types of nutrients. In order to stay healthy, the appropri-
16 ate amounts should be eaten every day from the five major food groups. The pyramid
17 suggests that people eat plenty of grains, vegetables, and fruit. Also, they should have
18 two to three servings from the milk group and two to three servings from the meat and
19 beans group. Representing the small tip of the pyramid, people should eat fats, oils, and
20 sweets sparingly.

21 The challenge is to choose nutritious foods. People need to know and follow the pyra-
22 mid to feel well, look good, and stay healthy.

GO ON

for **CHAPTER 22** page 644 continued

TEST

❶ Which of the following sentences is preferable to the one beginning, *When you eat,...* in line 1–2?

○ When you are supplying your body with the fuel for energy, you eat a bowl of cornflakes for breakfast.
○ While eating, you are supplying your body with energy fuel.
○ While supplying your body with energy, you can eat breakfast for fuel.
○ When you eat a bowl of cornflakes for breakfast, you are supplying your body with the fuel for energy.

❷ Which of the following should be added to the sentence beginning, *Energy is essential...* in line 2?

○ when you are growing.
○ that you like to do.
○ from tying your shoelaces to running a marathon.
○ from the beginning to the end.

❸ Which of the following is preferable to the words *is very important* in line 3?

○ will keep the body humming like a well-tuned engine.
○ is probably not as important as exercise.
○ may take a long time to figure out.
○ will give you enough energy to run the marathon.

❹ Which of the following sentences is preferable to the thesis in lines 3–4?

○ The USDA's MyPyramid simplifies and organizes the basics of good nutrition.
○ The USDA's MyPyramid explains how eating gives you energy.
○ Your body needs high energy foods for variety.
○ The information on the USDA's MyPyramid is too complicated to understand.

❺ Which of the following sentences is preferable to the one beginning, *The purpose of the pyramid...* in lines 6–7?

○ To follow the recommendations of the pyramid, eat better every day.
○ To eat better, people can follow the recommendations shown in the pyramid.
○ To help you eat better every day, the pyramid's recommendations should be followed.
○ To follow the recommendations is the purpose of the pyramid.

GO ON

CHAPTER 22 | Examining Causes and Effects | Writing Workshop

for **CHAPTER 22** page 644 continued   **TEST**

6 In the sentence beginning, *Unlike a car,...* which of the following changes should be made? (lines 9–11)

○ Unlike a car, the mechanical work of its muscles must be fueled while the body maintains itself.

○ Unlike a car, the body has to maintain itself in addition to fueling the mechanical work of its muscles.

○ Unlike a car, in addition to fueling the mechanical work of its muscles, the body has to maintain itself.

○ Unlike a car, the mechanical work of its muscles must be fueled and maintained by the body.

7 In the sentence, *In order to stay healthy, the appropriate number of servings should be eaten every day from the five major food groups.*, which of the following changes should be made? (lines 15–16)

○ In order to stay healthy, each of the five major food groups you should eat every day.

○ In order to stay healthy, people should eat the appropriate number of servings from each of the five major food groups every day.

○ In order to stay healthy, every day the appropriate number of servings should be eaten from each of the five major food groups.

○ In order to stay healthy, the five major food groups should be eaten from every day.

8 Which of the following is preferable to the sentence, *Representing the small tip of the pyramid, people should eat fats, oils, and sweets sparingly.*, in lines 19–20?

○ The small tip of the pyramid, representing fats, oils, and sweets, should be eaten sparingly.

○ At the tip of the pyramid, very few fats, oils, and sweets are represented.

○ Representing fats, oils, and sweets, the small tip of the pyramid lists foods people should eat sparingly.

○ Fats, oils, and sweets represent the small tip of the pyramid for eating sparingly.

9 Which of the following words should be added at the end of the sentence, *The challenge is...* in line 21?

○ that look and taste good.

○ from your favorite food groups.

○ that measure the energy that the body will use to fuel all its mechanical processes.

○ that balance the different nutrients the body needs for energy.

10 To clarify *why*, which of the following phrases should be placed at the beginning of the last sentence? (lines 21–22)

○ people need to know

○ and follow

○ follow the pyramid

○ to feel well, look good, and stay healthy

Reading Workshop: Problem-Analysis Article

DIRECTIONS *Read the following passage. Then read each question about the passage. Decide which is the best answer to the question. Fill in the bubble next to the answer you have chosen. Mark like this* ○ *not like this* ⊘ *.*

Changing Weather and Climate

In a 1961 television episode, a young woman suffers from 120-degree heat. The reason for her discomfort is a change in the earth's orbit, which is moving closer to the sun. At the end of the television episode, the woman wakes from a dream to discover that, in fact, the earth is moving *away* from the sun. This is a science fiction example of climatic change. In reality, scientific evidence suggests that there is a global warming trend, and the indisputable geologic record of ice ages indicates that the earth's climate does change. The results of such changes can have a tremendous impact on human life, disrupting peoples' food supplies, personal comfort, and choices of places to live.

The long-term state of the atmosphere in a particular location is called climate; the short-term state is called weather. Life and climate interact and alter each other, and this has occurred throughout history. Growing evidence indicates that the great societies of the Bronze Age collapsed because a severe dust storm brought on an extended drought, with resulting changes in climate. The Sahara Desert was once fertile and green. In the last century, the surface temperature of the earth has warmed about one degree, and a pattern of increased weather variability has been noted in recent years.

Significant weather changes are occurring throughout the world. For instance, La Niña, a cool trough of water in the Pacific Ocean, shifted the jet stream and funneled storms with heavy rainfall and snow to the Northwest and upper Midwest of the United States. At the same time, it left the Southwest much drier than usual. As weather patterns shift, the increase in floods, droughts, hurricanes, tornadoes, and extreme differences in temperature may alter people's lives drastically. An intense hurricane season in the Caribbean or dry summers in the wheat belt may result in economic hardships or personal tragedy.

Intense concern and debate revolves around global climate, especially global warming. Some scientists think the warming is a natural process with inherent cycles, while others claim that human action, such as burning fossil fuels and deforestation, is the major cause. The problem of global warming affects everyone, whether in urban areas with the aggravation of increased temperatures and smog or in agricultural environments with the uncertainty of harvests and destructive storms. Both public policies and individual efforts may lessen the effects of global warming.

Facing crop failure, property damage, or health issues, people are always concerned about the changeable nature of weather. This has led some scientists to study weather phenonoma and develop models to project the long-term effects of weather and climate. An increased ability to predict weather conditions before they occur has helped prevent many communication and transportation disasters. Meteorologists still seek methods with which to make more accurate and timely forecasts in order to preserve human life and resources.

The impact of rapidly changing weather patterns on human life may be overwhelming as living conditions, scarce resources, and economic conditions are altered. Because life and climate can transform each other, all people, not only scientists, must be vigilant and active to mollify the consequences of weather and climatic changes.

for **CHAPTER 23** *page 668* continued

TEST

1 Which of these would the author use to make a hasty generalization?
○ historical facts
○ an example from a television program
○ observations of weather disasters
○ a body of scientific evidence

2 Which fact supports the writer's generalization about weather patterns?
○ A television character suffers from extreme heat.
○ Ice ages show that the earth's climate changes.
○ La Niña affects weather in widespread regions.
○ Scientists study weather and its effects on people.

3 Which of these sentences states the problem addressed in the article?
○ Droughts are a weather phenomenon.
○ Extreme weather events are unpredictable.
○ Unexpected downpours occur.
○ Weather and climate changes impact people.

4 Which evidence of climatic change is given in the article?
○ the earth's orbit
○ communication problems
○ the end of the Bronze Age
○ damaged property

5 According to the article, which maybe a contributing factor to climatic change?
○ computer models
○ ravaging floods
○ the Sahara
○ burning fossil fuels

6 The statement that the surface temperature of the earth has warmed about one degree in the last century is relevant because —
○ temperature is a weather condition
○ it demonstrates a weather change
○ it indicates rising food supplies
○ it shows a particular measurement

7 The statement "the Sahara Desert was once fertile and green" is —
○ a fictional instance
○ a real world example
○ a statistic
○ a guess

8 In this article, the author focuses on —
○ the problem
○ the solutions
○ both problems and solutions
○ an analysis of causes

9 In the statement "people are always concerned about the changeable nature of weather," which word may make the generalization too broad?
○ nature
○ concerned
○ changeable
○ always

10 Which of the following is a suggested solution in the article?
○ better agricultural methods
○ attention to climatic changes
○ continued deforestation
○ more energy supplies

NAME	CLASS	DATE	SCORE

for CHAPTER 23 page 678

TEST

Writing Workshop: Problem-Analysis Essay

DIRECTIONS Read the following Problem-Analysis Essay. Some sections are underlined. The underlined sections may contain problems with one of the following:

- Content
- Organization
- Style
- Punctuation

Choose the best way to write each underlined section and mark the letter of your answer. If the underlined section needs no change, mark the choice "Correct as is."

Time to Help

We have to think about how we will spend our quality time both now (1) and later. We spend a good part of each weekday in school. Then there's (2) homework and helping out at home all the time. With weekends, vacations, and summers we have free time. What are we doing with that free time? Are we giving back to our communities? Are we helping others? We (3) are faced with so many responsibilities like homework and family issues. Most teenagers can find the time to volunteer and make the world a better place. It's as plain as the nose on your face. (4)

Some of us have jobs that take up hours of our time. Going to school means studying and doing homework. Playing sports requires time for practice and games. Playing a musical instrument also requires time. Not many of us use all our time for these activities. We find time to go to (5) movies, listen to music, chat on the Internet. Just hang out with our friends. It's great to have fun. It's important to have fun. However, if we fill our free time completely with fun, we are missing out on the rewards that (6) come from helping others.

We've all had the experience of getting help when we needed it. Often our families and friends help us. Not everyone has someone to ask for help. Environmental groups, hospitals, libraries, shelters, soup kitchens, (7) animal rescue groups, and retirement homes could all use our help. Many (8) communities have organizations that point volunteers in the direction that

GO ON

CHAPTER 23 | Analyzing Problems | Writing Workshop

61

for **CHAPTER 23** page 678 continued

TEST

best suits their abilities and interests. Volunteering gives someone else help when they need it. We can do more. More than we think we can.
(9)

I still want to listen to music and spend time with my friends, but I also want to give something of myself. A survey of teenagers showed that more of them volunteered when they were asked. We just need to be aware that volunteer opportunities are available. Volunteer work often leads to careers later on.
(10)

for CHAPTER 23 page 678 continued   TEST

1. A Our lives are so busy that we never seem to have enough time for everything we want to do.
   B There are many volunteer opportunities for students who do not participate in extracurricular activities.
   C We don't have much free time during the week because we spend so much time working on part-time jobs.
   D Correct as is

2. F We have to do homework and help out at home all the time.
   G Then there's homework and helping out at home.
   H Then there's homework. Helping out at home.
   J Correct as is

3. A An anonymous quote says we should volunteer.
   B Teenagers should volunteer instead of filling their free time with fun activities.
   C An anonymous quote says, "Volunteers don't necessarily have the time, but they have the heart."
   D Correct as is

4. F Put volunteering on your resume.
   G We need to make time to volunteer.
   H Time is important.
   J Correct as is

5. A We find time to go to movies, listen to music, chat on the Internet, and just hang out with our friends.
   B We find time to go to movies. Listen to music. Chat on the Internet. Just hang out with our friends.
   C We find time to go to movies and listen to music. Chat on the Internet and just hang out with our friends.
   D Correct as is

6. F we are missing out on the rewards.
   G we are missing out on the rewards of helping others and enjoying the experience.
   H we are missing out on the rewards of helping others.
   J Correct as is

7. A Groups that can use our help are hospitals and libraries.
   B There are many places we can help.
   C The list of places we can help is endless.
   D Correct as is

8. F Many communities have organizations that help volunteers.
   G Many communities point volunteers in the direction that best suits their abilities and interests.
   H Many communities have organizations that point volunteers in a direction.
   J Correct as is

9. A We can do more than we think. We can.
   B We can't do as much as we think we can, but we can try.
   C We can do more than we think we can.
   D Correct as is

10. F Taking the time to help will not interfere with other activities.
    G By taking the time to help, we can make a difference.
    H We should use our time more wisely.
    J Correct as is

Reading Workshop: Literary Analysis

DIRECTIONS *"The Necklace" by Guy de Maupassant is one of the most famous short stories ever written. In this passage a reviewer analyzes the story from a particular viewpoint.*

Fake Life or Fake Necklace?

The necklace was a fake, "worth only five hundred francs!" To Mme. Loisel, the main character of "The Necklace," the discovery of this simple fact about a showy piece of jewelry exposes a greater truth. Set in France in the 1800s, this story by Guy de Maupassant portrays the significance of social class and Mme. Loisel's discontent with her own position in society. The necklace symbolizes her materialism and shallow character, as the story's plot reveals her choices and their consequences.

2 A beautiful and charming woman, Mme. Loisel considers herself cheated because she cannot afford fine clothes, jewels, and a life of luxury. Blaming her discontent on her modest social status, Mme. Loisel exploits an opportunity to act for an evening as though she were wealthy. The evening is the undoing of the life—not luxurious, but comfortable—that she and her husband have.

3 When Mme. Loisel's husband receives an invitation to a society event, he sacrifices his own desires to provide his wife with money to dress for the occasion. She wants to attend in style. Not satisfied with an attractive evening gown, she thinks she will appear dowdy without jewels. Her husband indulges her by suggesting that she borrow some jewels from a wealthy friend—a fateful suggestion. The stage is set for Mme. Loisel's evening in high society. The evening satisfies Mme. Loisel's desire to be surrounded by luxury and to enjoy admiration. Her brief social success loses its glory, however, when she loses the elegant necklace on the way home.

4 For the next ten years, the expensive necklace the Loisels buy to replace the lost one dictates their every move. Loans taken out to buy the replacement must be repaid, requiring long hours of work and the giving up of even modest treats and comforts. The effort exhausts and disheartens them, and Mme. Loisel blames her fate on the capricious nature of life. After the loans have all been repaid, a chance meeting between Mme. Loisel and the wealthy friend who lent her the necklace reveals the simple truth. The necklace that Mme. Loisel borrowed was a fake. It would have cost only a small sum to replace if Mme. Loisel had told her friend that it was missing.

5 The showy, fake diamond necklace comes to represent the pretentious style of life for which Mme. Loisel was willing to sacrifice everything. How different her life might have been had she resisted the need to try to be something she was not! If only she had forgone that one elegant evening, she would not have sacrificed her basic comforts nor her husband's satisfaction with their simple lifestyle. Intent on finding a way for his wife to live out her fantasy, however, he, too, was partly responsible for the sad turn of events. In this cautionary tale, we are shown the hazards of not appreciating what we have and of aspiring to be what we are not.

NAME _____ CLASS _____ DATE _____

for **CHAPTER 24** *page 708* continued **TEST**

1. What would the author of this analysis probably say was the primary cause of Mme. Loisel's unhappiness?
   A a lie told by a wealthy friend
   B her husband's generosity
   C an invitation to an elegant party
   D her own envy

2. According to the writer, what is the purpose of the necklace in the story?
   F to create dialogue
   G to be a metaphor for life
   H to be a symbol of character
   J to establish a minor plot detail

3. What is the setting of "The Necklace"?
   A France in the 1700s
   B France in the 1800s
   C England in the 1800s
   D England in the 1700s

4. Why is the loss of the necklace at the close of the elegant evening significant?
   F It is a typical example of Mme. Loisel's behavior.
   G It determines a shift in the story's point of view.
   H It provides a turning point in the plot of the story.
   J It sets up a way of moving from one setting to another.

5. Which conclusion can you draw from the Loisels' actions regarding the lost necklace?
   A They had asked the wrong person about the value of the necklace.
   B They took responsibility for the loss as they perceived it.
   C They were afraid of being prosecuted for losing the necklace.
   D They forgot that the owner had told them the necklace was a fake.

6. Based on the analysis, which phrase best describes Mme. Loisel's personality at the beginning of the story?
   F polite but insincere
   G gracious but shy
   H content but lonely
   J hardworking but bitter

7. In this analysis, on which literary element does the author focus?
   A character
   B point of view
   C language
   D setting

8. Why does Mme. Loisel's husband go along with his wife's wishes?
   F He wants his wife to be happy.
   G He wants to be admired.
   H She offers him more money.
   J He thinks he can get a better job.

9. What purpose does Mme. Loisel's chance meeting of the wealthy friend at the end of the story serve?
   A It builds suspense.
   B It creates internal conflict.
   C It develops rising action.
   D It determines the plot resolution.

10. With which of the following statements would the author of this analysis probably agree?
    F Mme. Loisel's desires took her beyond her means.
    G Mme. Loisel would have been satisfied with just one elegant evening.
    H Mme. Loisel deserved more than she had in her life.
    J Mme. Loisel married a man who was not as worthy as she was.

CHAPTER 24 | **Analyzing a Short Story** | Reading Workshop

Writing Workshop: Literary Analysis

DIRECTIONS This is an early draft of a student essay. Some parts of the passage need to be rewritten. Read the passage and select the best answers for the questions that follow. Some questions are about particular sentences or parts of sentences and ask you to improve sentence structure and word choice. Other questions refer to parts of the essay or the entire essay and ask you to consider organization and development. In making your decisions, follow the conventions of standard written English. After you have chosen your answer, fill in the corresponding oval on your answer sheet.

(1) "I stake two million!" (2) "I stake my freedom!" (3) With these statements, the two main characters in Anton Chekhov's short story "The Bet" lay a reckless wager on the value of life. (4) Their extraordinary bet arises during an argument about capital punishment. (5) The bet is also nonsensical.

(6) The young lawyer says. "To live anyhow is better than not at all." (7) To prove it, he is willing to spend fifteen years alone in a room. (8) The wealthy banker feels that punishment by death is better than life in prison. (9) The banker holds the lawyer to his claim. (10) Under the terms of the bet, the lawyer will remain imprisoned for fifteen years. (11) As enhancements to his solitary existence, he will have only a musical instrument and any books he requests. (12) The banker will provide for the lawyer's needs during this time. (13) In addition, he will give the lawyer "two million" if the lawyer wins the bet.

(14) The strange bet is carried out, with the lawyer living in a guarded lodging on the banker's property. (15) The lawyer has survived his intense solitude by playing the piano and studying life through books. (16) He has learned six languages and studied philosophy, religion, history, natural science, and literature. (17) Instead of feeling enlightened, however, he has become ill, cynical, and hopeless.

(18) Two million was once a relatively small amount to the banker. (19) Two million is now a fortune he can't afford to lose. (20) "What is the good, he wonders, of that man's losing fifteen years of his life and my throwing away two million"? (21) On the eve of the bet's conclusion, the banker becomes panicked. (22) He decides to murder the prisoner in order to avoid paying the money. (23) The banker discovers the haggard, thin lawyer sleeping before a written account that says, "To prove to you in action how I despise all that you live by, I renounce the two million of which I once dreamed as of paradise and which now I despise." (24) The banker feels ashamed for his contemptible intentions. (25) The following day, before the appointed hour of completion, the lawyer silently leaves. (26) The banker secretly locks away the lawyer's written explanation.

(27) In "The Bet," Anton Chekhov shows us what happens when two people lay a wager on the value of life: No one wins.

1. To capture the reader's attention, which sentence should be added at the beginning of the analysis?

    (A) Do you think gambling is a good idea?
    (B) Two men were having a discussion.
    (C) Would you become a prisoner for money?
    (D) Life is not a game to be played frivolously.

2. In relation to the passage as a whole, what is the function of the first paragraph?

(A) To compare two similar characters from the story.
(B) To introduce the theme of the story.
(C) To sum up information that will be presented in the essay.
(D) To identify the author of the story.

3. Which of the following represents the best way to combine sentences 4 and 5 (reproduced below)?

Their extraordinary bet arises during an argument about capital punishment. The bet is also nonsensical.

(A) Their extraordinary bet arises, also nonsensical, during an argument about capital punishment.
(B) Their extraordinary bet arises during an argument about capital punishment, also nonsensical.
(C) Their extraordinary bet, and also a nonsensical bet, arises during an argument about capital punishment.
(D) Their extraordinary bet, which is nonsensical, arises during an argument about capital punishment.

4. Which of the following is the best revision, if any, of sentence 6 (reproduced below)?

The young lawyer says. "To live anyhow is better than not at all."

(A) The young lawyer says, "To live anyhow is better than not at all."
(B) "The young lawyer says To live anyhow is better than not at all".
(C) The young lawyer says, "To live anyhow is better than not at all".
(D) Make no change

5. Which of the following represents the best way to combine sentences 8 and 9 (reproduced below)?

The wealthy banker feels that punishment by death is better than life in prison. The banker holds the lawyer to his claim.

(A) The wealthy banker feels that punishment by death is better than life in prison or holds the lawyer to his claim.
(B) When the wealthy banker feels that punishment by death is better than life in prison, he holds the lawyer to his claim.
(C) The wealthy banker, who feels that punishment by death is better than life in prison, holds the lawyer to his claim.
(D) The wealthy banker feels that punishment by death is better than life in prison, and he holds the lawyer to his claim.

6. Which of the following sentences, if added after sentence 13, makes the most logical conclusion to the paragraph?

(A) At least the prisoner will be able to play music and read many interesting books.
(B) To win, the lawyer must remain in solitary confinement for the agreed-upon time.
(C) It is difficult for prisoners who have no choice but to stay in their cells alone.
(D) The lawyer believes that no matter how a person lives, it is better than no life at all.

for **CHAPTER 24** page 718 continued

TEST

7. Which of the following sentences, if added before sentence 18, best clarifies the plot?

   (A) The banker would later discover that the lawyer had become disdainful and renounced the bet.
   (B) Sometimes people plan devious actions that they might later regret but can never forget.
   (C) After nearly fifteen years, the banker has lost most of his money by taking too many risks.
   (D) When the prisoner was alone in his room, he probably missed the company of other people.

8. Which of the following represents the best way to combine sentences 18 and 19 (reproduced below)?

   Two million was once a relatively small amount to the banker. Two million is now a fortune he can't afford to lose.

   (A) Two million was once a relatively small amount for the banker to lose, but it is now a fortune he can't afford.
   (B) Two million is not only a fortune he can't afford, but was once a relatively small amount for the banker to lose.
   (C) Two million, to the banker, was once a rather small sum and to the banker is now a fortune he can't afford to lose.
   (D) Two million, which was once a relatively small amount to the banker, is now a fortune he can't afford to lose.

9. Which of the following represents the best revision of sentence 20?

   (A) "What is the good, he wonders, "of that man's losing fifteen years of his life and my throwing away two million?"
   (B) "What is the good," he wonders, "of that man's losing fifteen years of his life and my throwing away two million?"
   (C) "What is the good," he wonders, of that man's losing fifteen years of his life and my throwing away two million"?
   (D) "What is the good, he wonders, of that man's losing fifteen years of his life and my throwing away two million."

10. In relation to the passage as a whole, what is the function of the last sentence?

    (A) To conclude with a strong restatement of the thesis.
    (B) To suggest another reading of the story.
    (C) To revise an opinion that was stated earlier.
    (D) To offer the reader something to consider.

Reading Workshop: Research Article

DIRECTIONS The passage below is followed by questions based on its content. Answer the questions on the basis of what is <u>stated</u> or <u>implied</u> in the passage. Numbers 1–10 are based on the following passage.

United States' baseball players have not always had multimillion-dollar contracts. In the early years of the sport, many profes-
(Line) sional players took other jobs in the off-
(5) season. For years, baseball, the national pastime, was the favorite spectator sport. Large crowds paid to watch professional games, and the World Series was an exciting draw. Players and fans were aware that
(10) gamblers also liked baseball, but gambling on baseball was largely ignored. Charles Comiskey, the owner of the Chicago White Sox, declared, "To me, baseball is as honorable as any other business.... This year,
(15) 1919, is the greatest season of them all." By 1920, a gamble taken by some shady "businessmen" and a few players shook the honor of baseball.

In 1919, the Chicago White Sox were a
(20) winning team, but the players' pay was worse than that of players on losing teams. The World Series that year matched the White Sox against the Cincinnati Reds, with Chicago favored to win. Gamblers persuad-
(25) ed some disgruntled, underpaid White Sox players to make extra money by throwing the best-of-nine game series. The first baseman, after being approached by gamblers, recruited seven of his teammates to lose the
(30) World Series on purpose. Star hitter and outfielder Joe Jackson, better known as "Shoeless Joe," was among the eight men. Eliot Asinof's book, *Eight Men Out*, pulls together the details of what happened in
(35) 1919 and 1920.

Rumors that something was wrong reached sportswriter Hugh Fullerton even before the first game of the series. Chicago's players had superior baseball skills, but they
(40) were not known for good teamwork. Strangely, betting odds were shifting against Chicago. Fullerton and others scrutinized the games, looking for suspicious plays by the White Sox players. In the first game, sev-
(45) eral players fielded erratically, showed poor judgment, and made bad throws. The rumors seemed confirmed. However, the agreement between the gamblers and the eight players did not go well. Some of the
(50) players may have shown a change of heart. When the Reds were within one game of winning, Chicago made a comeback, winning several games. The gamblers intervened. Before there could be a ninth game,
(55) Cincinnati won the World Series.

It took almost a year for authorities—along with owners, players, and fans—to believe what had happened and act on the alleged wrongdoing in the 1919 World
(60) Series. On October 22, 1920, eight Chicago White Sox players were indicted for throwing the 1919 World Series. After months of legal processes, the eight men were tried in the courts of Illinois and acquitted by a jury.
(65) However, the following day they were banned from baseball forever by baseball officials. The baseball careers of the eight players, now known as the "Black" Sox, were over.

(70) Although the Black Sox scandal became a part of baseball history, baseball fans never wanted to believe that their beloved game of baseball could be tainted. The Chicago *Herald-Examiner* reported the words of a
(75) small boy seeing Shoeless Joe leave the grand jury room. "Say it ain't so, Joe," he pleaded. "Say it ain't so."

GO ON

for CHAPTER 25 *page 748* continued

TEST

1 Which of the following is the best paraphrase of the first two sentences of the passage?
(A) Baseball players have always made a lot of money, but now they make more.
(B) Baseball players used to have to work extra jobs because they did not get paid to play baseball.
(C) Baseball players used to work extra jobs because they did not make enough money playing baseball.
(D) Baseball players should have made more money but they did not.

2 Charles Comiskey's statement is most likely from a
(A) letter
(B) primary source
(C) textbook
(D) secondary source

3 In line 24, which of the following is the best paraphrase of the sentence beginning "Gamblers persuaded..."?
(A) Some of the players for the White Sox baseball team had a chance to make some money by throwing the World Series.
(B) Although they were disgruntled and underpaid, the White Sox players were happy to be in the World Series.
(C) Some of the baseball players for the White Sox team were unhappy and felt they were not paid enough money.
(D) Some of the players for the White Sox were unhappy because they were not making enough money. Gamblers gave them a chance to make money by throwing the World Series.

4 The writer of this article refers to the book *Eight Men Out* by Eliot Asinof as
(A) an endorsement
(B) a primary source
(C) a historical document
(D) a secondary source

5 In line 38, which of the following is the best paraphrase of the sentence beginning "Chicago's players..."?
(A) The Chicago team played with excellent baseball skills but poor teamwork.
(B) The Chicago team was better than the Cincinnati team.
(C) The Chicago White Sox was the better team because of their baseball skills.
(D) The Chicago team had players with superior baseball skills, so they were better than the Cincinnati team.

6 The writer's descriptions of Hugh Fullerton's actions are most likely from
(A) an interview
(B) a speech
(C) an article
(D) a tape recording

7 In line 56, which of the following is the best paraphrase of the first two sentences?
(A) A year after the World Series, an investigation was begun about wrongdoing on the part of the White Sox.
(B) A year after the 1919 World Series, Cincinnati was declared the winner.
(C) As the result of an investigation a year later, eight White Sox players were accused of having thrown the series.
(D) It took almost a year for an investigation into the 1919 World Series to be started.

GO ON

for **CHAPTER 25** page 748 continued   TEST

8 Which of the following is the best paraphrase of the two sentences in lines 62–67?

(A) The players were not convicted for gambling, but they were banned from baseball forever.
(B) The players were convicted for gambling and banned from baseball forever.
(C) The players were not convicted for gambling, and their baseball careers resumed.
(D) The players were not convicted for gambling, and baseball officials were relieved.

9 The quote, "Say it ain't so, Joe" is most likely from

(A) an encyclopedia
(B) an eyewitness account
(C) a magazine
(D) a biography

10 Which of the following is the best paraphrase of the last paragraph of the passage?

(A) The Black Sox scandal is part of baseball history.
(B) The Chicago *Herald Examiner* reported all of the details of the Black Sox scandal.
(C) No one ever believed that the Black Sox scandal had occurred.
(D) Even the youngest baseball fans did not want to believe that the Black Sox scandal had occurred.

CHAPTER 25 | Sharing Research Results | Reading Workshop

Writing Workshop: Research Paper

DIRECTIONS Read the following research paper. Some sections are underlined. The underlined sections may contain problems with one of the following:

- content
- organization
- style
- punctuation

Choose the best way to write each underlined section and mark the letter for your answer. If the underlined section needs no change, mark the choice "Correct as is."

Three Points in Contact

Climbing has become trendy, and some people like the challenge and satisfaction of conquering the rocks. (1) That can be a huge boulder, a towering frozen waterfall, or a mountain face that rises higher than the eye can see. (2)

The first climbers did not scale mountains for sport. They climbed for a view of the land below. John Muir climbed to commune with nature. (3) (Achey) Most modern-day climbers climb simply for sport. Today, climbing involves sophisticated equipment, competitions, and indoor climbing walls.

The sport of climbing is a test of an individual's physical and mental strength, but it is important for individual climbers to rely on one another for safety and support on rock and ice. (4) Rock climbing requires ropes that are attached to climbers and threaded through carabiners, or metal rings. (5) It is best to have an experienced climber set up the ropes and lead.

A climber relies on eyes, hands, and feet for climbing. Generally hands are used for balance, feet for support, and eyes for spotting holds. The most important climbing rule is "three points in contact," meaning that two hands and a foot or two feet and one hand must always be touching the rock. Maintaining balance, one hand or foot moves on the rock. (6)

Climbing gyms are the safest places to climb indoors. (7) Routes are configured for different (8) types of climbs, and inclement weather is not a problem. Considered by some to be the best (9) female rock climber, Katie Brown practices her holds and moves in simulated conditions during the week, but "on weekends," she says, "I like to experience real rock climbing" (Walters). Brown enjoys her celebrity as a famous climber. (10)

1. A Although climbing has become trendy, its true appeal is the challenge and satisfaction of conquering the object of the climb.
   B There are those who buy the clothes and gear for climbing and never use them because they are out of fashion.
   C Its true appeal is the companionship of other climbers who tend to think, dress, and behave alike.
   D Correct as is

2. F It can be a boulder, a frozen waterfall, or a mountain face.
   G That can be a towering boulder, a waterfall frozen in winter, or a mountain most people would not dare to scale.
   H That can be a boulder that stands 30 feet high, a frozen waterfall that drops 40 feet, or a mountain face that rises more than 9000 feet.
   J Correct as is

3. A Some people climbed to commune with nature (Achey).
   B John Muir climbed to commune with nature (Achey).
   C John Muir climbed mountains (Achey).
   D Correct as is

4. F In the sport of rock climbing, individual climbers must rely on one another for safety.
   G The sport of rock climbing tests an individual's physical and mental strength for safety.
   H In the sport of rock climbing, individual climbers' physical and mental strength is tested by nature, and individual climbers must rely on one another for safety and support when they climb on rock and ice.
   J The sport of climbing is a test of an individual's physical and mental strength. Nevertheless, climbers must rely on one another for safety and support on rock and ice.

5. A Rock climbing requires ropes that are long and strong that are attached to climbers and threaded through carabiners.
   B Rock climbing requires ropes and carabiners to ensure safety in case of a fall.
   C Rock climbing requires ropes for safety as well as carabiners, or metal rings.
   D Rock climbing requires ropes that are attached to climbers and threaded through carabiners, or metal rings, to ensure safety in case of a fall.

GO ON

CHAPTER 25 | Sharing Research Results | Writing Workshop

73

for **CHAPTER 25** page 758 continued

TEST

6 F Maintaining balance, the climber moves one hand or foot, reestablishes the three points in contact before moving the next hand or foot, and slowly progresses along the rock.
   G Maintaining balance, one hand or foot moves, and the climber progresses along the rock.
   H Maintaining balance, one hand or foot moves, reestablishes the three points in contact before the next hand or foot moves, then the climber reestablishes the three points of contact and progresses along the rock.
   J Correct as is

7 A Climbing gyms indoors are the safest places to climb.
   B Gyms are the safest indoor places to climb.
   C Indoor climbing gyms are the safest places to climb.
   D Correct as is

8 F Routes are configured so that climbers do not have to try new moves.
   G Safety makes it difficult to configure routes that people will use in inclement weather.
   H Most safe climbers come to climbing gyms only in inclement weather.
   J Correct as is

9 A Considered by some to be the best female rock climber, Katie Brown practices on weekends, but "I like to experience real rock climbing" (Walters).
   B Considered by some to be the best female rock climber, Katie Brown practices her holds and moves in simulated conditions during the week. She says, "On weekends I like to experience real rock climbing" (Walters).
   C Katie Brown practices her holds and moves during the week, but on weekends "I like to experience real rock climbing" and is considered one of the best (Walters).
   D Correct as is

10 F Brown is recognized wherever she climbs, in a climbing gym or on a mountain.
   G Brown's enthusiasm exemplifies the climber's love of a challenge and sense of conquest.
   H Brown is modest about her collection of medals and citations.
   J Correct as is

Reading Workshop: Persuasive Article

DIRECTIONS Read the persuasive article "It's Not News to Me" before answering questions 1 through 10.

IT'S NOT NEWS TO ME

News today inundates our lives. We are bombarded by the media through the Internet, television, radio, magazines and even quaint newspapers. It is easy today to find information and news reports about things happening halfway across the world. However, how do we know the information we are getting is factually correct and unbiased? The question of bias and factual basis as well as misrepresentation or harmful reporting is a difficult one. What should be done to make sure news sources report news accurately and responsibly? We should create a national news council to oversee the work of the news media. A news council, a self-governing body made up of members of the media and the public, holds public hearings on complaints against the media. The council determines by a vote whether someone has been harmed or misrepresented by a newspaper or television story and reports that decision.

Weekly newspapers first appeared in the early 1600s; dailies followed about a hundred years later. The advent of radio newscasts and newsreels shown in movie theaters in the first half of the twentieth century provided additional access to the news, and television news debuted in the 1950s. Today, a wide range of news media exists, including all-news cable television stations, print publications, and on-line sources.

Increased accessibility to the public does not decrease journalistic responsibility. To fill twenty-four hours of news time, news editors must present a variety of stories, although it seems unnatural for every news medium to focus on one sensational scoop—be it a politician's personal scandal or a murder. At times, journalists seem to fixate on stories they think are popular or will bring ratings needed to maintain advertising support. The news media can fixate on any story as long as it is presented in a fair and accurate manner. News councils can't tell the networks what stories to cover, but they can make sure the media gets the facts straight.

News councils have been established to promote accuracy, balance, and fairness in journalism. The Minnesota News Council started in 1970. Several other states now have news councils or are considering establishing them. Industry councils provide a means of self-regulation. For example, the legal, medical, financial, and advertising industries all have them. Some journalists themselves recognize the need for councils in the media.

A news council can address questions of fairness without burdening the legal system, guide the media to present appropriate news stories, and allow the media and the public to listen to and learn from each other. An effective news council will make sure the media tells us the truth.

for **CHAPTER 26** page 792 continued **TEST**

1 What type of persuasive technique is used in the second sentence?
  A. logical appeal
  B. emotional appeal
  C. opinion statement
  D. speculation

2 What strong opinion is expressed in this article?
  F. Some journalists are opposed to news councils.
  G. Increased availability to the news increases journalistic freedom.
  H. News councils should be established to keep the news media honest.
  I. Sensational news items attract attention.

3 The statement that television news debuted in the 1950s is
  A. an implied opinion.
  B. a convincing reason.
  C. a specific fact.
  D. an argument.

4 Which phrase from the article signals an opinion?
  F. should create
  G. often present
  H. has been adopted
  I. are considering

5 Which word BEST represents loaded language?
  A. journalistic
  B. bombarded
  C. appropriate
  D. establishing

6 The statement, "At times, journalists seem to fixate on stories . . ." is an opinion because it
  F. gives a specific example.
  G. cannot be argued.
  H. tells the source of the information.
  I. gives information that cannot be proven true.

7 Which phrase most likely stirs the reader's feelings?
  A. personal scandal
  B. journalistic responsibility
  C. advertising support
  D. means of self-regulation

8 The statement, "The Minnesota News Council started in 1970," is a fact because it
  F. can be argued.
  G. cannot be debated.
  H. tells where the information was found.
  I. gives information that cannot be verified.

9 Why is the statement, "Some journalists themselves recognize the need . . . " for news councils a fact?
  A. It includes a generalization clue.
  B. It includes a value word.
  C. Proof for this information can be found.
  D. It tells the source of the information.

10 The last paragraph of this article is BEST described as
  F. a prediction opinion.
  G. an emotional appeal.
  H. an expert opinion.
  I. a logical appeal.

Writing Workshop: Persuasive Essay

DIRECTIONS *The following persuasive essay was written by a student who just graduated from high school. Read the passage (which may contain some errors) and answer the questions that follow. Be sure to fill in the bubble next to the answer you choose. Mark like this ○ not like this ⌀. You may look back at the passage as you answer questions.*

Don't Wait Until You Graduate

1   It's a big world out there. You're going to have to make money to pay for basics, to
2   have fun, and to get ahead. Start thinking about career possibilities. If you wait until
3   you graduate, you won't hardly know what you're going to do, what the best job for
4   your abilities is, or even what kind of education and training you need. Your decisions
5   will be based on panic and uncertainty.

6   There are many opportunities in school to investigate different careers. Schools often
7   sponsor career days, internships, vocational-technical training, and work-study pro-
8   grams. Other ways to find out about careers include volunteering, taking aptitude tests,
9   and interviewing people about their jobs. Your school's guidance center probably has
10 career information, and the Web and libraries can be searched. Keep a record of your
11 ideas, findings, and responses to the information.

12 If career research sounds time-consuming, don't do it. You can't wait until a few weeks,
13 or even a few months, before you graduate. You can always get information when you
14 need it, even if it means doing volunteer work some place like a retirement community.
15 It is also a good idea to find out about a career that seems interesting and then consider
16 it for a while in order to decide whether it is something you really want to do. On the
17 other hand, it's not scarcely advisable to decide on a career path too early and close the
18 door on possibilities. Keep researching and thinking about your career options. You
19 should try to make an informed and thoughtful decision about your future.

20 Adults usually are willing to help high school students learn about careers. Use their
21 help and ideas. You do not necessarily have to do what they say, but you can always
22 listen and add their advice to all the other information you find. The bottom line is that
23 you do not want to make no major decision about your career because you need a job
24 immediately or because you have too little information. Decide where you want to go
25 to college before you start planning your career.

for **CHAPTER 26** page 803 continued

TEST

① Which of the following questions should be added to the first paragraph in line 2?

○ How do schools help with career awareness?
○ How do you prepare for the "real world"?
○ How do computers help with career awareness?
○ How do you prepare for an aptitude test?

② Which of the following changes should be made?

○ Change **won't** to **will not** (line 3)
○ Delete **hardly** (line 3)
○ Change **you're** to **you are** (line 3)
○ Delete **going** (line 3)

③ Which of the following sentences is preferable to the one beginning, *Your decisions will be...* in lines 4–5?

○ Your decisions will not be as good.
○ Your decisions will be from panic and uncertainty.
○ You will base your decisions on panic and uncertainty.
○ You will be more prepared to make decisions.

④ Which of the following sentences is preferable to the one beginning, *Your school's guidance center...* in lines 9–10?

○ Your school's guidance center can be searched for career information.
○ Your school's guidance center probably has career information, and the Web and libraries are places that can be searched for information.
○ You can be searching your school's guidance center, the Web, and libraries.
○ Your school's guidance center probably has career information, and you can search the Web and libraries.

⑤ Which of the following sentences is preferable to the one beginning, *If career research...* in line 12?

○ Time-consuming research can be eliminated if you don't panic.
○ If career research sounds time-consuming, that's because it is.
○ If researching and thinking about your career options makes you tired, just keep going.
○ Don't take time to do time-consuming research because you will have more time when you get a job.

GO ON

78 ELEMENTS OF LANGUAGE | Fourth Course | *Chapter Tests in Standardized Test Formats*

NAME _____ CLASS _____ DATE _____

for **CHAPTER 26** page 803 continued

TEST

6 Which of the following sentences is preferable to the one beginning, *You can always get...* in lines 13–14?

○ Technology provides a wide array of career possibilities.
○ Unless you stumble into a lot of money, you're going to have to work.
○ Waiting until the last minute may give you the chance to visit many job sites to see what people actually do at work.
○ At the last minute, it is impossible to put in enough volunteer time at a retirement community to find out if you might like a career working with seniors.

7 Which of the following changes should be made in line 17?

○ Change **not scarcely** to **not hardly**
○ Change **not scarcely** to **not**
○ Change **not scarcely** to **certainly**
○ Change **too early** to **much too early**

8 Which of the following changes should be made?

○ Change **use** to **utilize** (line 20)
○ Change **use** to **ignore** (line 20)
○ Change **use** to **take advantage of** (line 20)
○ Change **ideas** to **assistance** (line 21)

9 Which of the following changes should be made in line 23?

○ Change **do not** to **do**
○ Change **do not** to **don't hardly**
○ Delete **decision**
○ Change **no major** to **a major**

10 Which of the following sentences is preferable to the one beginning, *Decide where you want...* in lines 24–25?

○ Use the time while you are in school to prepare yourself for the job market.
○ Plan to take all the advice you get from parents, teachers, and counselors.
○ Some careers require technical training, but you have to look into employment after you finish school.
○ Most careers are built on lucky breaks, but it never hurts to do some serious investigation into careers.

CHAPTER 26 | Persuading Others | Writing Workshop

NAME	CLASS	DATE	SCORE

for CHAPTER 27 page 836

TEST

Reading Workshop: Persuasive Brochure

DIRECTIONS *You have probably been handed brochures in many places, such as the street and tourist offices. Do you really look at them and read them? Read and study the following inside and back panels of a persuasive brochure. Then answer the questions that follow.*

[Inside Panel]

PLANT A TREE

Plant trees to enjoy, honor, and protect your environment.

Ah, the joys of sitting under a cool shade tree, sipping a glass of lemonade on a hot summer's day. Trees are a pleasant addition to any community, but there are many more practical reasons to plant trees.

Here's how and why planting trees will help your community:

Trees . . .

- absorb dust and heat
- act as windbreaks
- reduce glare so that cities and towns do not become "heat islands"
- supply food such as nuts, fruits, and berries and ingredients for medicines
- produce oxygen and reduce carbon dioxide
- increase atmospheric moisture

"The cultivation of trees is the cultivation of the good, the beautiful, and the ennobling . . ."

—J. Sterling Morton

[Back Panel]

Celebrate Arbor Day each year. This very special holiday was founded in 1872 by J. Sterling Morton in Nebraska.

Here's how and why to help plant trees in your community:

Plant Trees . . .

- to celebrate Arbor Day, Earth Day, Tu B'Shebat, a birth, a birthday, an anniversary, a baptism or confirmation, or any other special occasion
- in memory of someone special
- to contribute to a healthy environment
- to save energy
- to support birds and wildlife
- to improve community pride

Contact . . .

- the National Arbor Day Foundation
- your local forestry service
- a business organization that sponsors tree-planting
- the national Plant-It organization

Put down some roots.

GO ON

80 ELEMENTS OF LANGUAGE | Fourth Course | *Chapter Tests in Standardized Test Formats*

NAME _____ CLASS _____ DATE _____

for CHAPTER 27 page 836 *continued*

TEST

1. The description of sitting under a shade tree and sipping lemonade is an example of which of the following?
   A bandwagon technique
   B emotional words
   C a glittering generality
   D name-calling

2. To what is the image of a tree in this brochure most likely to draw your attention?
   A reasons for planting trees
   B ways to plant trees
   C holidays that celebrate planting trees
   D ways to find tree-planting contacts

3. Which of the following best describes J. Sterling Morton's quote?
   A plain folks
   B testimonial
   C logical appeal
   D intense words

4. Why is the text set in boxes at the bottom of the inside panel and the top of the back panel?
   A The boxes help the reader predict which information is important.
   B The boxes give the reader a sense of warmth.
   C The boxes draw the reader to the text inside them.
   D The boxes encourage the reader's eye to slow down.

5. On the back panel what is the purpose for the list of reasons to plant trees?
   A The list transfers positive qualities of people to trees.
   B The list transfers positive qualities of trees to people.
   C The list focuses on the concept of peace.
   D The list provides persuasive evidence.

6. Which of the following best describes the function of the leaf image on the back panel?
   A breaks up text
   B adds color
   C symbolizes work
   D draws attention to key words

7. What is the purpose of this brochure?
   A to persuade readers to buy a product
   B to convince readers to support a cause
   C to provide information about trees
   D to tell a personal experience

8. The other panels of this brochure are most likely to include which of the following?
   A reasons to plant flowers
   B reasons to buy trees
   C more information about tree planting
   D more information about wildlife

9. In evaluating the visual elements of this brochure, which would be the *least* important aspect to consider?
   A headings
   B graphics
   C type sizes
   D sentence length

10. In what way does the font most likely affect the reader?
    A reinforces important dates
    B slows down reading
    C draws attention to major points
    D distracts reader from factual information

CHAPTER 27 | Using Persuasion in Advertising | Writing Workshop   81

Writing Workshop: Persuasive Brochure

DIRECTIONS Read the following inside and back panels of a persuasive brochure. Then read each question after the brochure. Choose the best answer. Then mark the space for the answer you have chosen.

[Inside Panel]

WHY VOTE?

Your vote really can make a difference. Many elections for congress have come down to just a handful of votes.

You may be on the fence about voting. The reasons *to* vote are better.

Not To Vote	To Vote
• I don't really care about the election.	✓ It's your basic right as a citizen.
• My vote doesn't really count.	✓ It's your way to have a voice in how things work.
• One more vote either way isn't going to make a difference in the final outcome.	✓ Voting gives you choices.
• I'm not registered.	✓ Registering to vote is easy.

The United States of America is a democracy—<u>founded and uphold</u> on rights and freedoms for all people. Voting is one of those rights. Each time you vote, YOU—as a U.S. citizen—are acknowledging and upholding democracy.

[Back Panel]

HOW DO I VOTE?

You won't be able to cast your vote until you are registered. Here are some of the ways you can register to vote:

- Contact your local election office—you can register by mail.
- Be a motor voter—register when you get or renew your driver's license.
- Go to register at a library or another designated place.
- Look for a voter registration drive at a community event, local college, or shopping mall.

Once you are a registered voter, be prepared to vote. Know the candidates and the issues.

- Watch the news for information.
- You will want to vote.
- Look for Web sites on the candidates and issues.
- Listen when the candidates <u>debated</u>.
- Try to remember to vote in the next election.

Still think your vote won't count? Believe it or not, your vote counts.

GO ON

for **CHAPTER 27** page 846 continued

TEST

❶ Which of these applies to the top section of the inside panel?

A The text should be replaced with a photograph.
B The slogan for the brochure is repeated in the text.
C An illustration would give more information than the text.
D The heading and text introduce the information in the section.

❷ You may be on the fence about voting.

How is this sentence best written?

A You may be undecided about voting.
B For every reason *not to* vote, there is a reason *to* vote.
C You may not be sure about voting.
D *As it is*

❸ Which subheading should be added to the chart on the inside panel?

A Why you should vote
B Why votes count
C Take a look
D Reasons to vote

❹ The United States of America is a democracy—founded and uphold on rights and freedoms for all people.

How should founded and uphold be written?

A found and uphold
B founded and upheld
C found and upheld
D *As it is*

❺ Which of the following subheadings should be added just before the last paragraph on the inside panel?

A What are my choices?
B Why do I register?
C How do I vote?
D Still not convinced?

❻ You will want to vote.

Which of the following best replaces this sentence?

A Look for information on voter registration.
B Voting is fun.
C Vote at your local election office.
D Study political brochures.

❼ Listen when the candidates debated.

How should debated be written?

A will debate
B did debate
C debate
D *As it is*

❽ Try to remember to vote in the next election.

Which of the following best replaces this sentence?

A Ask questions if you get a chance to meet a candidate.
B If you get a chance, think about voting.
C Try to remember to find out about candidates.
D Try to remember to ask candidates questions.

GO ON

for CHAPTER 27 page 846 continued

TEST

9 | Believe it or not, your vote counts.

Which is the best substitute for this cliché?

A Believe it or not, you'll be glad you voted.
B You'd better believe your vote will count.
C Count on this: Your vote won't count unless you do.
D Your vote will count.

10 Which of these best describes the last section of the back panel?
A catchy slogan
B call to action
C logical argument
D visual element

CHAPTER 16: Correcting Common Errors
Standardized Test Answer Sheet

Most standardized tests require that you use a No. 2 pencil. Each mark should be dark and completely fill the intended oval. Be sure to completely erase any errors or stray marks. If you do not have a pencil, follow your teacher's instructions about how to mark your answers on this sheet.

1

Your Name: _____
(Print)   Last   First   M.I.

Signature: _____

Class: _____ Date: ___/___/___
(Print)   Month Day Year

2 Your Name — First 4 Letters of Last Name | First Init. | Mid. Init. (A–Z bubbles)

3 Date — Month (Jan.–Dec.), Day, Year

4 Grade

5 Age

For each new section, begin with number 1. If a section has more answer spaces than questions, leave the extra spaces blank.

Grammar and Usage Test

Section 1 — Questions 1–15, choices A B C D E

Section 2 — Questions 1–15, choices A B C D E

Mechanics Test

Section 1 — Questions 1–15, choices A B C D E

Section 2 — Questions 1–15, choices A B C D E

NAME _____ CLASS _____ DATE _____ SCORE _____

Answer Sheet 1
Chapter _____

Grammar, Usage, and Mechanics

1. Ⓐ Ⓑ Ⓒ Ⓓ
2. Ⓐ Ⓑ Ⓒ Ⓓ
3. Ⓐ Ⓑ Ⓒ Ⓓ
4. Ⓐ Ⓑ Ⓒ Ⓓ
5. Ⓐ Ⓑ Ⓒ Ⓓ
6. Ⓐ Ⓑ Ⓒ Ⓓ
7. Ⓐ Ⓑ Ⓒ Ⓓ
8. Ⓐ Ⓑ Ⓒ Ⓓ
9. Ⓐ Ⓑ Ⓒ Ⓓ
10. Ⓐ Ⓑ Ⓒ Ⓓ

NAME _____ CLASS _____ DATE _____ SCORE _____

Answer Sheet 2
Chapter _____

Sentences and Paragraphs

1. Ⓐ Ⓑ Ⓒ Ⓓ
2. Ⓕ Ⓖ Ⓗ Ⓙ
3. Ⓐ Ⓑ Ⓒ Ⓓ
4. Ⓕ Ⓖ Ⓗ Ⓙ
5. Ⓐ Ⓑ Ⓒ Ⓓ
6. Ⓕ Ⓖ Ⓗ Ⓙ
7. Ⓐ Ⓑ Ⓒ Ⓓ
8. Ⓕ Ⓖ Ⓗ Ⓙ
9. Ⓐ Ⓑ Ⓒ Ⓓ
10. Ⓕ Ⓖ Ⓗ Ⓙ

11. Ⓐ Ⓑ Ⓒ Ⓓ
12. Ⓕ Ⓖ Ⓗ Ⓙ
13. Ⓐ Ⓑ Ⓒ Ⓓ
14. Ⓕ Ⓖ Ⓗ Ⓙ
15. Ⓐ Ⓑ Ⓒ Ⓓ
16. Ⓕ Ⓖ Ⓗ Ⓙ
17. Ⓐ Ⓑ Ⓒ Ⓓ
18. Ⓕ Ⓖ Ⓗ Ⓙ
19. Ⓐ Ⓑ Ⓒ Ⓓ
20. Ⓕ Ⓖ Ⓗ Ⓙ

ELEMENTS OF LANGUAGE | Fourth Course

NAME _____ CLASS _____ DATE _____ SCORE _____

Answer Sheet 3

Chapter _____

Sentences and Paragraphs

1. Ⓐ Ⓑ Ⓒ Ⓓ
2. Ⓐ Ⓑ Ⓒ Ⓓ
3. Ⓐ Ⓑ Ⓒ Ⓓ
4. Ⓐ Ⓑ Ⓒ Ⓓ
5. Ⓐ Ⓑ Ⓒ Ⓓ
6. Ⓐ Ⓑ Ⓒ Ⓓ
7. Ⓐ Ⓑ Ⓒ Ⓓ
8. Ⓐ Ⓑ Ⓒ Ⓓ
9. Ⓐ Ⓑ Ⓒ Ⓓ
10. Ⓐ Ⓑ Ⓒ Ⓓ
11. Ⓐ Ⓑ Ⓒ Ⓓ
12. Ⓐ Ⓑ Ⓒ Ⓓ
13. Ⓐ Ⓑ Ⓒ Ⓓ
14. Ⓐ Ⓑ Ⓒ Ⓓ
15. Ⓐ Ⓑ Ⓒ Ⓓ
16. Ⓐ Ⓑ Ⓒ Ⓓ
17. Ⓐ Ⓑ Ⓒ Ⓓ
18. Ⓐ Ⓑ Ⓒ Ⓓ
19. Ⓐ Ⓑ Ⓒ Ⓓ
20. Ⓐ Ⓑ Ⓒ Ⓓ

NAME _____ CLASS _____ DATE _____ SCORE _____

Answer Sheet 4
Chapter _____

Reading Workshop

1 Ⓐ Ⓑ Ⓒ Ⓓ   5 Ⓐ Ⓑ Ⓒ Ⓓ   9 Ⓐ Ⓑ Ⓒ Ⓓ
2 Ⓕ Ⓖ Ⓗ Ⓙ   6 Ⓕ Ⓖ Ⓗ Ⓙ   10 Ⓕ Ⓖ Ⓗ Ⓙ
3 Ⓐ Ⓑ Ⓒ Ⓓ   7 Ⓐ Ⓑ Ⓒ Ⓓ
4 Ⓕ Ⓖ Ⓗ Ⓙ   8 Ⓕ Ⓖ Ⓗ Ⓙ

Writing Workshop

1 Ⓐ Ⓑ Ⓒ Ⓓ   5 Ⓐ Ⓑ Ⓒ Ⓓ   9 Ⓐ Ⓑ Ⓒ Ⓓ
2 Ⓕ Ⓖ Ⓗ Ⓙ   6 Ⓕ Ⓖ Ⓗ Ⓙ   10 Ⓕ Ⓖ Ⓗ Ⓙ
3 Ⓐ Ⓑ Ⓒ Ⓓ   7 Ⓐ Ⓑ Ⓒ Ⓓ
4 Ⓕ Ⓖ Ⓗ Ⓙ   8 Ⓕ Ⓖ Ⓗ Ⓙ

ELEMENTS OF LANGUAGE | Fourth Course

NAME _____ CLASS _____ DATE _____ SCORE _____

Answer Sheet 5

Chapter _____

Reading Workshop

1	Ⓐ Ⓑ Ⓒ Ⓓ	5	Ⓐ Ⓑ Ⓒ Ⓓ	9	Ⓐ Ⓑ Ⓒ Ⓓ
2	Ⓐ Ⓑ Ⓒ Ⓓ	6	Ⓐ Ⓑ Ⓒ Ⓓ	10	Ⓐ Ⓑ Ⓒ Ⓓ
3	Ⓐ Ⓑ Ⓒ Ⓓ	7	Ⓐ Ⓑ Ⓒ Ⓓ		
4	Ⓐ Ⓑ Ⓒ Ⓓ	8	Ⓐ Ⓑ Ⓒ Ⓓ		

Writing Workshop

1	Ⓐ Ⓑ Ⓒ Ⓓ	5	Ⓐ Ⓑ Ⓒ Ⓓ	9	Ⓐ Ⓑ Ⓒ Ⓓ
2	Ⓐ Ⓑ Ⓒ Ⓓ	6	Ⓐ Ⓑ Ⓒ Ⓓ	10	Ⓐ Ⓑ Ⓒ Ⓓ
3	Ⓐ Ⓑ Ⓒ Ⓓ	7	Ⓐ Ⓑ Ⓒ Ⓓ		
4	Ⓐ Ⓑ Ⓒ Ⓓ	8	Ⓐ Ⓑ Ⓒ Ⓓ		

NAME _____ CLASS _____ DATE _____ SCORE _____

Answer Sheet 6
Chapter _____

Reading Workshop

1 Ⓐ Ⓑ Ⓒ Ⓓ   5 Ⓐ Ⓑ Ⓒ Ⓓ   9   Ⓐ Ⓑ Ⓒ Ⓓ
2 Ⓕ Ⓖ Ⓗ Ⓘ   6 Ⓕ Ⓖ Ⓗ Ⓘ   10 Ⓕ Ⓖ Ⓗ Ⓘ
3 Ⓐ Ⓑ Ⓒ Ⓓ   7 Ⓐ Ⓑ Ⓒ Ⓓ
4 Ⓕ Ⓖ Ⓗ Ⓘ   8 Ⓕ Ⓖ Ⓗ Ⓘ

Writing Workshop

1 Ⓐ Ⓑ Ⓒ Ⓓ   5 Ⓐ Ⓑ Ⓒ Ⓓ   9   Ⓐ Ⓑ Ⓒ Ⓓ
2 Ⓕ Ⓖ Ⓗ Ⓘ   6 Ⓕ Ⓖ Ⓗ Ⓘ   10 Ⓕ Ⓖ Ⓗ Ⓘ
3 Ⓐ Ⓑ Ⓒ Ⓓ   7 Ⓐ Ⓑ Ⓒ Ⓓ
4 Ⓕ Ⓖ Ⓗ Ⓘ   8 Ⓕ Ⓖ Ⓗ Ⓘ

ELEMENTS OF LANGUAGE | Fourth Course

Notes

Notes

Notes

Notes

Notes